Cooking Light
First Foods

©2010 by Time Home Entertainment Inc.
135 West 50th Street, New York, NY 10020

ISBN-13: 978-0-8487-3321-6
ISBN-10: 0-8487-3321-5
Library of Congress Control Number: 2009937176
Printed in the United States of America
First Printing 2010

Oxmoor House

VP, Publishing Director: Jim Childs
Editorial Director: Susan Payne Dobbs
Brand Manager: Terri Laschober Robertson
Senior Editor: Heather Averett
Managing Editor: Laurie S. Herr

Cooking Light® First Foods

Editor: Rachel Quinlivan, R.D.
Project Editor: Diane Rose
Senior Designer: Melissa Jones Clark
Director, Test Kitchens: Elizabeth Tyler Austin
Assistant Director, Test Kitchens: Julie Christopher
Test Kitchens Professionals: Allison E. Cox, Julie Gunter, Kathleen Royal Phillips, Catherine Crowell Steele, Ashley T. Strickland
Photography Director: Jim Bathie
Senior Photo Stylist: Kay E. Clarke
Associate Photo Stylist: Katherine Eckert Coyne
Production Manager: Theresa Beste-Farley

Contributors

Writer: Carolyn Land Williams, M.Ed., R.D.
Contributing Editor: Shannon McRae
Medical Consultant: Linda J. Stone, MD
Compositor: Susan Dendy
Copy Editor: Norma Butterworth-McKittrick
Proofreader: Lauren Brooks
Fact-Checker: Barry Wise Smith
Indexer: Mary Ann Laurens
Interns: Sarah Bélanger, Chris Cosgrove, Georgia Dodge, Perri K. Hubbard, Ina Ables, Maggie McDaris, Allison Sperando

Test Kitchens Professionals: Telia Johnson, Amy Liscomb, Connie Nash, Angela Schmidt
Photographers: Lee Harrelson, Becky Luigart-Stayner

Cooking Light®

Editor: Scott Mowbray
Creative Director: Carla Frank
Deputy Editor: Phillip Rhodes
Food Editor: Ann Taylor Pittman
Special Publications Editor: Mary Simpson Creel, M.S., R.D.
Nutrition Editor: Kathy Kitchens Downie, R.D.
Associate Food Editors: Timothy Q. Cebula, Julianna Grimes
Associate Editors: Cindy Hatcher, Brandy Rushing
Test Kitchen Director: Vanessa T. Pruett
Assistant Test Kitchen Director: Tiffany Vickers Davis
Senior Food Stylist: Kellie Gerber Kelley
Recipe Testers and Developers: SaBrina Bone, Deb Wise
Art Director: Fernande Bondarenko
Deputy Art Director: J. Shay McNamee
Junior Deputy Art Director: Alexander Spacher
Photo Director: Kristen Schaefer
Senior Photographer: Randy Mayor
Senior Photo Stylist: Cindy Barr
Photo Stylist: Leigh Ann Ross
Copy Chief: Maria Parker Hopkins
Assistant Copy Chief: Susan Roberts
Research Editor: Michelle Gibson Daniels
Editorial Production Director: Liz Rhoades
Production Editor: Hazel R. Eddins
Art/Production Assistant: Josh Rutledge
Administrative Coordinator: Carol D. Johnson
CookingLight.com Editor: Allison Long Lowery

Cover: large baby image: Fuse/Getty Images; toddler with peas: UpperCut Images Photography/Veer; baby with spoon: Corbis Photography/Veer; Green Peas puree (page 29); Banana-Mango Frozen Yogurt (page 118)

Back Cover: Honey-Glazed Carrots (page 77); Pumpkin Dip (page 83); Mac and Cheese with Roasted Tomatoes (page 66); Sunshine Smoothie (page 120); Yellow Cake with Chocolate Frosting (page 135)

To order additional publications, call 1-800-765-6400 or 1-800-491-0551.
For more books to enrich your life, visit **oxmoorhouse.com**
To search, savor, and share thousands of recipes, visit **myrecipes.com**

Cooking Light
First Foods

Oxmoor House®

Contents

Welcome to *Cooking Light First Foods*—the first-ever cookbook from *Cooking Light* created especially for babies and toddlers!

Introducing foods to your baby is an exciting adventure, but it's one that is often filled with questions. Being a registered dietitian, I naively assumed that feeding my first child would be stress free. I kept up on current research, taught cooking classes, and counseled adults and children about healthy eating. What else was there to know? But when it was time to introduce solids to my own baby, I found myself bombarded with advice from well-meaning friends and family. When I followed the research and facts that I knew, Madeline's first meals became much more enjoyable experiences for both of us. Madeline is now almost 3 years old, and sitting around the dinner table is my family's favorite time of the day.

The first few chapters of this book will walk you through introducing foods into your child's diet during his or her first year of life and answer questions that all parents have at mealtimes, such as when to introduce foods and how much to feed your baby. The second half focuses on expanding baby's palate and keeping mealtime a happy, nutritious experience. All of the recipes in *Cooking Light First Foods* were tested in our Test Kitchens, approved by registered dietitians, and sampled by our Baby and Toddler Tasting Panel to help ensure that each recipe is flavorful and nutritious.

Cooking Light First Foods was created not only to provide tasty, nutritious recipes for babies and toddlers, but also to help simplify mealtimes for moms and dads by showing you how to slowly introduce baby into family meals. My hope is that this book will help your mealtimes become some of your family's favorite times, too!

Carolyn Land Williams
Mom of Madeline, age 2½ years

the essentials

Baby's First Foods

The sleepless nights, countless diapers, and constant questions are finally behind you. You're getting used to being a parent and feel settled into your routine—and now it's time for baby to start solid food. Bombarded with recommendations from other mothers, relatives, baby books, and magazines, it's no surprise that new moms get overwhelmed. But don't panic. Feeding your baby can be an exciting and rewarding experience—and a perfect opportunity to spend some family time together.

getting started

Though you've probably heard stories of toddlers refusing to eat anything but chicken nuggets, mealtime doesn't have to be stressful. The goal of *Cooking Light First Foods* is to **simplify mealtime** and make feeding less intimidating. We're not here to pressure you. Instead we offer nutritious recipes and snack suggestions that you can use to feed baby extensively or with commercial baby foods.

Building blocks of nutrition

Good nutrition is particularly important during baby's first year for proper growth and development. But there's another reason to make sure baby eats well early in life: Infants who are taught good nutrition from the start will be one step ahead in developing healthy practices for a lifetime.

During the first year, baby's primary source of nutrition will be breast milk or formula, but beginning at age 4 to 6 months, solid foods can be introduced. As baby's eating capabilities expand, the kind of foods that parents offer should expand as well. Too often, parents fall into a rut of fixing the same things because it's easy. But it's important to offer variety in your baby's diet. It's also crucial for parents to practice the good nutrition habits they want their children to develop. Like everything else you'll teach your child, what you *do* matters more than what you *say*.

homemade baby foods

Pros:
- Control over quality of ingredients
- Wider variety of foods
- Can be made in bulk
- Less expensive
- Less waste

Cons:
- Requires preparation time and some equipment
- Requires some storage space if making in bulk

commercial baby foods

Pros:
- Quick
- Convenient

Cons:
- Less control over ingredients
- Fewer food varieties
- Packaging waste
- More expensive

Why make your own baby food?

Although it does require a little more planning and time in the kitchen, making your own baby food provides several benefits.

- **Economics:** When made in batches (making more than one serving and storing extra for later), homemade baby food definitely saves you money. One large sweet potato costs an average of $1 and yields about three to four servings for baby. Four jars of baby food will cost you around $2 (even more if you buy organic versions). This cost difference adds up when you consider how much food your baby will eat during the next nine months or so.
- **Environment:** Homemade food produces very little waste since there's no packaging or labels. Plus, making food at home removes the energy-consuming steps of bottling, packing, and shipping commercial products

to your local store. We encourage you to shop at your local farmers' market for in-season produce for freshness and flavor.

- **Health:** Making food gives you complete control over what your baby eats, which means you can avoid preservatives, colorings, and fillers that have no nutritional benefit. This can be especially important if your child has food allergies or is at risk for developing them.

- **Variety and exposure:** The possibilities for purees and dishes are limited only by your creativity. Rather than sticking to the basics offered on the baby-food shelf at the store, you can expose baby to a larger variety of tastes and textures when you make the food yourself. Some research has indicated that exposure to a wide variety of textures and tastes by age 1 helps make the transition to table food easier.

Is homemade food right for you and your baby?

Millions of children have been nourished and have thrived on store-bought baby food, and you aren't less of a mother if you decide not to make every bite of food from scratch. There are pros and cons to both homemade and commercial foods, and only you know what is best for you and your child.

The good news is that it doesn't have to be an all-or-nothing decision. Maybe you start by making a few simple purees and decide it's very easy. Or perhaps during busy weeks of balancing work with an older sibling's soccer games, feeding baby store-bought food is the best answer for your sanity. Either way, you've already made an important step by carefully considering the importance of what your baby eats.

introducing foods

Introducing new tastes to baby is an exciting time for parents, but it often comes with lots of questions. Below is a general timetable of when to introduce foods.

When to introduce foods

0 to 4 months
- Breast milk or formula

4 to 6 months

Begin to Add:
- Single-grain cereals (rice, oat, and barley)
- Single-vegetable purees
- Single-fruit purees

6 to 8 months

Continue to Add:
- Single-grain cereals (rice, oat, and barley)
- Single-vegetable purees
- Single-fruit purees

Then Add:
- Mixed grain-and-vegetable purees
- Mixed grain-and-fruit purees
- Simple fruit-and-vegetable combinations

8 to 12 months

Add:
- Chunkier purees
- Proteins (meat, poultry, fish, and tofu purees; cheese; and yogurt)
- Very soft finger foods

1 year

Add:
- Eggs
- Whole cow's milk
- Finger foods
- Mixed dishes cut into small pieces and served with a spoon

Wean:
- Formula
- Baby purees

---

nutrition notes

avoiding honey

*H*oney can be a great natural sweetener— but only after baby's first birthday. The American Academy of Pediatrics warns that honey should not be given or added to any food or beverage for a child under age 1 because it can contain botulism spores, which produce toxins that can cause food poisoning in babies. Adults and babies over age 1 are able to fight off these toxins, but young babies are not. This warning even includes honey in baked goods; only very high temperatures kill botulism spores, and baked products often don't reach temperatures high enough to kill the spores.

Food allergies

Allergic reactions can occur anytime a person is introduced to something new. If the body perceives the new substance as a threat, the immune system produces antibodies to fight it off—even if the substance is completely harmless. Reactions tend to occur quickly after the food is eaten or when the person comes in contact with the food. The symptoms can range from mild to severe.

It can be scary and unsettling to see your child experience a reaction. Your pediatrician or allergist is always your best resource if your child has any kind of reaction to food. Below are the recommendations on how to prevent possible food allergies.

food allergy symptoms

- Breathing problems and throat tightening
- Swelling of eyes, lips, and/or tongue
- Sneezing and wheezing
- Rashes or hives
- Persistent diarrhea or abdominal pain
- Vomiting

How to avoid food allergies

The American Academy of Pediatrics offers these tips to fight off allergies:
- Wait until age 4 to 6 months to introduce solid foods.
- Introduce one new food at a time; wait four days before introducing another. During this time, watch for any signs of allergic reactions. Consult your pediatrician if a reaction occurs.
- Most of the common foods that trigger allergic reactions (see list at right) are safe to introduce to older infants and toddlers. However, consult your pediatrician or allergist before doing so, especially if baby has a parent or sibling with a food allergy.

most common foods that trigger an allergic reaction

- Cow's milk and dairy products
- Eggs
- Fish and shellfish
- Tree nuts (walnuts, pecans, etc.)
- Citrus fruits and berries
- Peanuts
- Soy
- Wheat

Food intolerances

Food intolerances, or food sensitivities, are often confused with food allergies because the symptoms are similar, but milder. Food intolerances, however, are not true allergies because the body doesn't produce antibodies. Intolerances can be triggered by foods that a person has trouble digesting such as milk, wheat, or soy or food additives and preservatives. If baby has a food sensitivity, discontinue serving that food for a few months, and then introduce it again. Parents often find that the food is tolerated well after baby's digestive tract and immune system have been given further time to mature.

The good news about both food allergies and sensitivities is that many children outgrow them by age 5, according to the American Academy of Pediatrics.

food intolerance symptoms

- Eczema, skin rashes, and hives
- Runny nose or sudden congestion
- Dark circles under eyes or puffy red eyes
- Bloating, diarrhea, or excessive gas

get cooking

Congratulations! You've made the decision to give making your own baby food a try. The next eight pages will walk you through all you need to know about choosing ingredients and equipment as well as preparing and storing the food.

Ingredients for success

- **Select good produce:** Select the same kind of produce for baby that you would choose for yourself—ripe and blemish free. Unripe fruit is often too sour or acidic and won't taste good to baby.
- **Avoid salt and sugar:** As hard as it may be, *do not add sugar or salt to baby's foods.* Your infant's kidneys aren't able to process adult levels of sodium, and baby simply does not need added sugar. New foods and textures are intriguing enough for baby, and the natural sweetness of foods provides plenty of flavor.
- **Open your mind:** When preparing food for your little one, be willing to try unusual combinations and foods that might not be your favorites. As adults, we've developed beliefs about what is and is not appetizing. But babies are uninfluenced by these beliefs, and they often love combinations of food that adults may think sound unappetizing.

at our house

Putting aside food preferences

One of my biggest hurdles was putting aside my own food preferences and opinions. Without realizing it, I found myself flipping past recipes because they used a food I didn't care for or wasn't familiar with. It was my duty as a good mother to serve Madeline only delicious, appetizing foods, right? And surely she has food preferences similar to mine, right?

My "breakthrough" came when I was at the house of a friend who had a daughter around the same age, and I saw her feeding her baby a dinner mixture of mashed avocado, rice cereal, and bananas. I literally cringed as she offered to prepare the same for Madeline, but I gave in. To my surprise, Madeline ate it all and loved it! I realized right then that I had to keep my food preferences separate when feeding Madeline. Just because I thought avocado was an "adult" food and the banana-avocado-cereal combo sounded bizarre, I had been limiting Madeline both in nutrients and exposure to new healthy foods.

—Carolyn Williams, *Cooking Light First Foods* author and mom of Madeline, 2½ years

Understanding organics

You've decided to try your first batch of baby food, and you head to the store for your ingredients. Now comes another choice—organic or not? Grocery stores everywhere are filling up fast with "organic" products. Though the term is often associated with better quality—and more expensive—produce and food, what does it really mean, and do you need to splurge on organic varieties for your baby?

What does "organic" mean?

In 2002, the U.S. Department of Agriculture (USDA) implemented uniform standards for American organic farmers and manufacturers. Organic foods must be grown or produced without chemical pesticides or fertilizers, and, for livestock, without the use of antibiotics or growth hormones. Organic foods cannot be genetically modified, irradiated, or cloned. Further guidelines govern specific foods. For instance, organic chickens must be raised with outdoor access.

So any foods you buy that carry the USDA green-and-white "certified organic" label have met the USDA's criteria for containing ingredients that are 95 to 100 percent organic. Whole foods (such as an apple) must be 100 percent organic. For mixed foods (such as a can of soup) at least 95 percent of the ingredients must be organic.

---

nutrition notes

best produce to buy organic

apples	nectarines
bell peppers	peaches
carrots	potatoes
celery	spinach
cherries	strawberries
lettuce	

Organic on a Budget

There's a cost to pay for organic foods because most tend to be more expensive than their non-organic counterparts. There is no clear, direct answer about the long-term effect of pesticides and hormones on humans, but when you think about feeding your baby, going organic and avoiding chemicals as much as possible seems like a good choice.

So how do you make healthy baby foods on a budget? Certain produce retains more pesticides and chemical residue than others, according to the Environmental Working Group, a nonprofit organization that uses public information to protect public health and the environment. We suggest you spring for organic varieties of the fruits and vegetables listed above when possible, as well as organic poultry, meat, and dairy.

---

fresh vs. frozen

*F*resh is best, right? Not necessarily. Most frozen fruits and vegetables are just as nutritious as fresh because they are frozen soon after being picked, so few nutrients are lost. Organic varieties are also available. Although frozen often can't compete with the vibrant flavors and textures of ripe fresh produce, it does provide convenience and similar nutrients.

the tools

You don't have to make any big investments to prepare foods properly for baby. In fact, you probably already have most of the necessary equipment in your kitchen.

Processing tools

You'll need at least one of the following pieces of equipment to prepare purees for baby.

Fork or potato masher

pros:
- Easy, quick, inexpensive, and portable
- Best for naturally soft foods like avocado or banana

cons:
- Does not make most purees as smooth and pureed as baby needs for first feedings

Cost: $2–$10

Food mill

pros:
- Easy, inexpensive, and good for smooth consistency for first purees
- Purees and strains
- Manual power rather than electric

cons:
- Uses manual hand power

Cost: $20–$150

Food processor or blender

pros:
- Easy, quick, and a variety of speeds and blades
- Larger capacity good for bulk preparation

cons:
- More expensive brands usually do a better job
- Doesn't work well for single servings

Cost: $20–$200

There are a variety of
affordable options to prepare
food for baby.

Magic Bullet

pros:
- Easy, quick, and small
- Good for single servings or bulk (has 12-ounce, 20-ounce, and 48-ounce capacity cups)

cons:
- Expensive
- May leak if not put together correctly

Cost: $100

Williams-Sonoma Beaba Babycook

pros:
- Steams, purees, warms, and defrosts all in one
- Good for single or small servings

cons:
- Expensive
- Maximum capacity is 2½ cups

Cost: $150 plus additional accessories

Other useful tools and supplies

We found that these additional tools made preparation easier in our kitchens. They are not required, but they are helpful—and you probably already have them.

Steamer basket
why it's helpful:

These porous stainless steel baskets hold fruits and vegetables just above the boiling water in a saucepan to perfectly steam produce. Cost: $8–$25

Strainer
why it's helpful:

When preparing some of baby's first fruit and vegetable purees, it's sometimes difficult to remove all the lumps and make the puree as smooth as baby wants. A quick fix: smooth out lumpy purees by pushing them through the strainer using the back of a spoon. The strainer will also catch any tough fibers or seeds. Cost: $3–$15

the essentials

pureeing 101

Cook times and methods will differ slightly depending on the food, but you can use this simple process to prepare most fruits, vegetables, meats, and grains for baby.

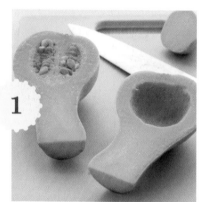

1. Prep.

Wash or peel produce; cut the food into smaller pieces.

2. Cook.

Steam, boil, or bake the food until it's very tender.

3. Puree.

Process or mash the cooked food until it's smooth or until desired consistency is reached.

4. Strain.

Spoon the food through a fine strainer or sieve to smooth the lumps and remove unprocessed parts of produce (this step may or may not be required).

5. Portion.

Spoon the puree into single-serving dishes or storage containers; serve the puree to baby. Store it promptly for later use.

storing food

One of the keys to making the process less time-consuming is to prepare baby's foods in bulk. You'll notice that the majority of our recipes store well for future use. As you learn what foods baby prefers, try doubling or tripling the recipes to store in the freezer. We recommend storing foods in single servings to help ensure food safety and simplify mealtime for you.

storing in refrigerator

Shelf life: up to two days
Best storage method: Portion food into clean, empty glass baby food jars with lids or individual serving containers with lids (a).

storing in freezer

Shelf life: up to three months
Best storage method: Freeze in ice-cube trays (b) or as "splats" on a wax paper–lined cookie sheet (c); once frozen, store in an airtight container, and label the container with the date and name of the food. Or store large portions in small freezer-safe bags; once thawed, portion the food into servings, and refrigerate. To make it easy to find the recipes in this book that freeze well, we've marked them with a small blue snowflake. ❄

a

b

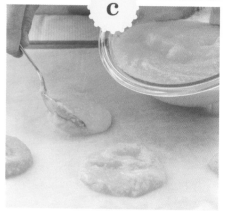

c

Safe thawing

Make sure you follow one of the methods below to ensure that baby's food is kept safe when defrosting and reheating. Heating is often unnecessary by the time a food is fully defrosted. Remember, baby does not have the expectation that food should be hot when served, and room temperature will usually be most palatable. You should serve the food to baby within 48 hours after it is defrosted. Discard any servings that are not used within that time.

- **Defrost in the refrigerator:** Place frozen puree cubes or "splats" into baby's serving dish, cover, and place in the refrigerator overnight.
- **Water bath:** Place sealed frozen bags of purees in a warm water bath; replace the water as needed. Once defrosted, portion the food into individual bowls, cover, and refrigerate until serving.

- **Defrost the food in the microwave:** Place frozen puree cubes or "splats" into a microwave-safe dish, and cook using the DEFROST setting on the microwave. Stir and rotate the food often. Make sure the food is completely cool before serving.

a note on sanitation

Proper sanitation and hygiene are essential when you're preparing food for baby. Follow these tips to keep the food and baby safe.

- Wash your hands before handling food and before feeding baby.
- Thoroughly clean all of the equipment and utensils. (Use the sanitizing cycle on your dishwasher to help ensure thorough cleaning.)
- Keep surfaces and cutting boards clean. Wash cutting boards in between cutting different foods.

- Toss any food servings that baby has eaten from.
- Toss any uneaten food that baby's spoon has touched.
- Discard any opened refrigerated homemade food and commercial food after two days. Often the food may not smell or look bad, but it is not safe to give to baby.

Weaning Baby

First bites are a big milestone in baby's life. You're probably eager to see your little one's reaction to solid food, and you'll more than likely snap a few photos of the messy moment. But if you're left wondering what to do next when the excitement of the first feeding is over, you're not alone.

making the transition

The transition from breast milk or formula to solid foods is a big one, and lots of parents have questions. Read on for answers to common concerns and quick tips for making those first months of food fun.

When should you introduce solid foods?

Everyone has an opinion on when your baby should start solid foods. While older relatives might insist that adding cereal to a bedtime bottle early on in baby's life would guarantee a good night's sleep, research suggests otherwise. Most babies are ready for solid food between 4 and 6 months of age, according to the American Academy of Pediatrics. Prior to 4 months of age, babies' digestive tracts are still too immature to fully breakdown and absorb the nutrients in solids, so it's important not to start too early.

The exact timing of when you start solids simply depends on when you think your baby is ready. By 6 months, babies need the additional nutrition that solids provide. This is particularly true for breastfed babies who at 6 months need the additional iron and zinc available in iron-fortified cereals and pureed meats.

nutrition note

how to introduce foods

Here is a step-by-step guide to introducing foods. We recommend making notes of each food you introduce, how baby liked it, and any reactions to the food.

1. Pick a single-grain infant cereal, such as rice, or a single-fruit or vegetable puree (see recipes starting on page 28), and prepare it. Cereals should be prepared with breast milk or formula.

2. Serve the same food to baby for at least four days, watching for any signs of allergy or intolerance.

3. Move on to a new food, and start the process over until baby has tried a variety of single foods.

The signs baby is ready for solids

You don't want to rush to introduce solids if baby isn't ready, so how do you know? One tip-off is the loss of baby's tongue-thrust reflex. In the first few months of life, this reflex protects baby from choking by using the tongue to push objects out of the mouth. Until baby outgrows this reflex, feeding solids can be pointless since most food will fall out of baby's mouth. You'll also know it's time to start solids when your baby:

- Is between 4 and 6 months
- Has good control of his or her head and can sit well when supported
- Has outgrown the tongue-thrust reflex and is able to swallow food
- Still acts hungry after 6 to 8 breastfeeding sessions or 32 ounces of formula per 24-hour period
- Has doubled his or her birth weight
- Is curious about what you are eating

Is there a particular order for introducing foods?

Most people start with a single-grain cereal, such as rice cereal, followed by single vegetables and then fruits. According to the American Academy of Pediatrics, however, there's no scientific evidence that introducing foods in this particular order provides any benefit to baby. While the sequence doesn't matter, it is important to introduce foods one at a time so that you can monitor any intolerances or allergies. Once baby has been exposed to many different foods, offer fruits and vegetables of all colors on a daily and weekly basis so he'll get a variety of flavors and nutrients. Simple combinations (like peas and carrots) shouldn't be offered until you're certain that baby can tolerate both foods in the mixture.

green

avocado ● broccoli

kiwifruit ● green beans

green peas ● asparagus

zucchini

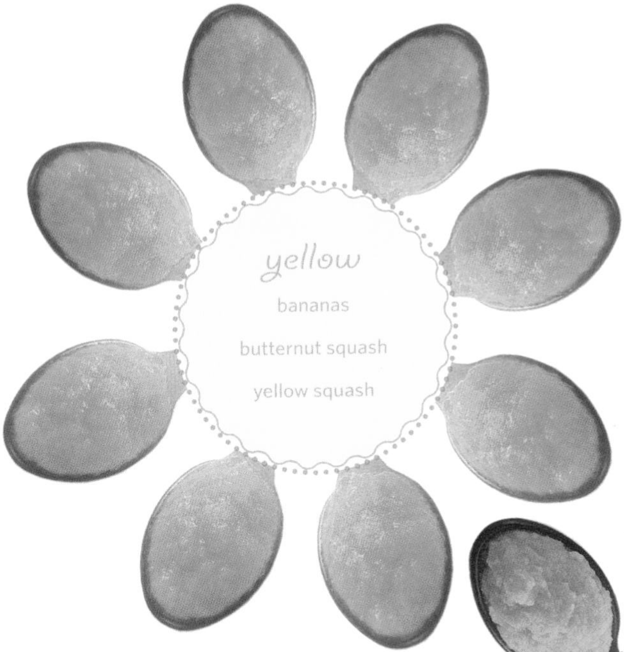

yellow

bananas

butternut squash

yellow squash

nutrition note

early sweet tooth?

Some parents worry that if babies taste sweeter foods first, they'll develop a "sweet tooth" and reject their veggies. In fact, you'll still see occasional recommendations to feed baby only vegetables (instead of fruit) at first because of this thinking—even though research hasn't proven this theory to be true. Several of our First Purees recipes (page 28) are made with sweet vegetables or fruit. This is because root vegetables and soft fruits are mild in flavor and make smooth purees, which babies tend to find more palatable.

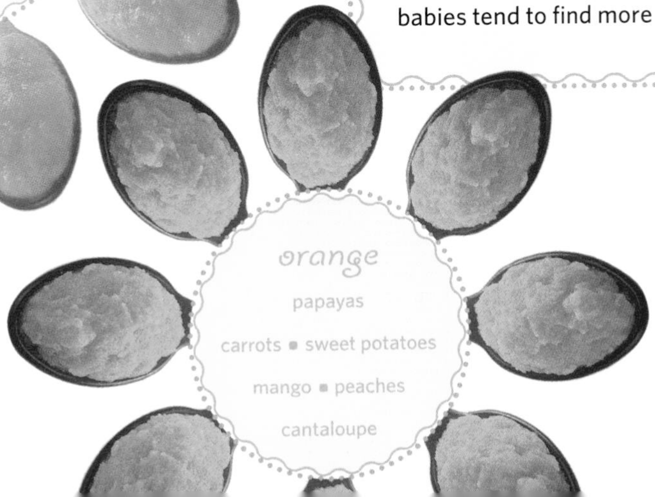

orange

papayas

carrots ● sweet potatoes

mango ● peaches

cantaloupe

red and purple

dried plums • plums
beets

How do you fit solids into baby's normal feeding schedule?

You might feel like baby's feeding schedule will be thrown off with the addition of a new meal even if it is just a few bites of rice cereal, but it won't. The purpose of baby's solid "meal" at this stage is really to teach him how to eat, not to sustain him nutritionally. Many parents find it easiest to start that first meal in between two established milk feedings.

   Below we offer two sample feeding charts. Feel free to adapt them to your baby's needs and schedule. The charts are meant to serve only as examples of how you incorporate a solid meal into baby's usual milk feedings. Always follow your pediatrician's advice; each baby is unique and may have slightly different needs than what we recommend.

Thick or thin?

Until now, baby has been on a liquid diet, so solids will present a new texture that your little one might not like at first. Start out by offering baby very smooth purees that almost pour off the spoon. This thin consistency will help make the transition from liquid to solid meals easier. As baby gets the hang of eating from a spoon and manipulating solids in his mouth, you can start serving thicker purees. Hold off on chunkier solids that have more texture until baby reaches 8 months. Though chunkier food won't necessarily harm him, he'll likely spit out anything with an unfamiliar texture.

It's still (mostly) all about the milk.

Even as baby begins eating solids, breast milk or formula will still serve as her primary source of nutrition during the 4- to 6-month period. Most babies should be receiving about 28 to 32 ounces of formula or breast milk a day during this stage—the same or not much less than what baby had before starting solids. While solids provide some calories and nutrients, the small amounts aren't enough to sustain her.

sample feeding chart for baby just starting solids

Early Morning	Morning	Late Morning to Noon	Early to Mid-Afternoon	Early Evening	Bedtime
Approximately 4-8 oz baby's milk	1-2 Tbsp. rice cereal*	Approximately 4-8 oz baby's milk	Approximately 4-8 oz baby's milk	Approximately 4-8 oz baby's milk	Approximately 4-8 oz baby's milk

feeding chart for baby a few weeks after starting solids

days 1–4

Early Morning	Morning	Late Morning to Noon	Early to Mid-Afternoon	Early Evening	Bedtime
Approximately 4–8 oz baby's milk	2-4 Tbsp. Sweet Potatoes*	Approximately 4–8 oz baby's milk	Approximately 4–8 oz baby's milk	Approximately 4–8 oz baby's milk	Approximately 4–8 oz baby's milk

days 5–8

Approximately 4–8 oz baby's milk	2-4 Tbsp. Green Beans*	Approximately 4–8 oz baby's milk	Approximately 4–8 oz baby's milk	Approximately 4–8 oz baby's milk	Approximately 4–8 oz baby's milk

*It's fine to feed baby solid food more than once per day. If you'd like to, feed baby before or after early evening feeding. Just make sure it's the same food you served earlier in the day while introducing foods.

How much should baby eat?

At first your baby may eat 1 to 2 tablespoons at a meal. Baby will gradually eat more solids over the next few months— ½ cup (4 ounces) or more. There's no magic formula on how much your baby needs. Some will eat more, and some will eat less, so watch your baby for cues. Serve baby food with an infant-sized rubber-tipped spoon, and make bites small, not heaping.

How do you know when baby is full?

Baby's appetite will vary, so the amount he eats may change daily. Don't force it—just continue to offer the food at the next meal. As baby gets used to solid foods, he'll eat more. A few signs that baby may have had enough to eat include:

• Turns head away from spoon
• Becomes uninterested in eating; plays with spoon
• Leans back in chair or seat
• Refuses to open mouth

Keys to successful first feedings

• **Timing is everything:** Plan to offer solid food when baby is well rested, happy, and not yet completely starving. Don't be surprised if your fussy, hungry baby rejects her green beans. Remember, this is a big change for baby. Working with her schedule will make feedings smoother for everyone.

• **Start with a calm(er) house:** Choose a time when your home is calm and there are few(er) distractions. This will help both you and your baby focus on mealtime.

• **Don't get upset:** Feedings during this age (and really for the next year) aren't glamorous and are often messy, so be prepared for mealtimes to not always go smoothly. Don't get upset if baby spits out the food, refuses to eat, or makes a huge mess. This is a new learning experience for everyone. Mealtimes will get easier.

first purees

These purees are perfect for baby's first encounter with solid food. They tend to be popular with baby because they are smooth, mild-flavored, and slightly sweet. Remember to thin them down to an almost liquid consistency for baby's first few meals.

Carrots ❊

Babies love carrots, which are full of beta carotene that helps keep growing eyes healthy.

1   pound carrots (about 6 carrots), peeled and cut into ½-inch-thick slices

1. Place carrot in a vegetable steamer. Steam, covered, 20 minutes or until very tender. Remove carrot from steamer, reserving cooking liquid. **2. Place** carrot in a food processor; process until smooth, adding cooking liquid, 1 tablespoon at a time, to reach desired consistency. **Yield:** 1½ cups or 6 (¼-cup) servings.

Bananas

Bananas don't keep well, so we recommend cutting off just the amount of fruit baby will eat prior to peeling. Store remaining unpeeled banana in a covered container, and serve it at the next meal.

½   ripe banana, peeled
1   tablespoon water, formula, or breast milk

1. Mash banana with a fork, adding 1 tablespoon water, formula, or breast milk to reach desired consistency. Serve immediately. **Yield:** about ½ cup or 2 (¼-cup) servings.

❊ *Denotes recipes that freeze well.*

Avocado

Avocados are a great portable option for baby when dining out. Use a dinner knife to halve an avocado, reserve one half in a plastic bag, and serve the remaining half to baby. Ripe avocados are usually soft enough to scoop out each bite and serve to baby using the skin as the serving bowl.

1   avocado, halved
2   tablespoons water, formula, or breast milk

1. Scoop out flesh from one avocado half; reserve avocado half with pit for a later use. Mash avocado with a fork, adding 2 tablespoons water, formula, or breast milk, 1 tablespoon at a time, to reach desired consistency. Serve immediately. **Yield:** ½ cup or 2 (¼-cup) servings.

easy freezing

These recipes are based on ¼-cup serving sizes. If you freeze batches in ice-cube trays, one cube usually holds 2 tablespoons. We recommend defrosting just one cube when baby is new to solid food. Later on when baby has started eating more, defrost two to four cubes (2 to 4 ounces or ¼ to ½ cup).

Green Peas ❊

Peas may thicken slightly and stick together after they're refrigerated. To loosen them, stir in a small amount of water, formula, or breast milk when reheating.

1   (16-ounce) package fresh or frozen petite green peas, thawed

1. Place peas in a vegetable steamer. Steam, covered, 6 minutes or until very tender. Remove peas from steamer, reserving cooking liquid. **2. Place** peas in a food processor; process until smooth, adding cooking liquid, 1 tablespoon at a time, to reach desired consistency. Strain using a sieve or food mill, if needed; discard solids. **Yield:** 1½ cups or 6 (¼-cup) servings.

Butternut Squash ❊

Babies usually love acorn and butternut squash because of their naturally sweet flavor and smooth, velvety consistency. Follow the same directions to make acorn squash.

1   small butternut squash (about 1 pound)
Cooking spray
1   tablespoon water (optional)

1. Preheat oven to 400°. **2. Cut** squash in half lengthwise; remove seeds and membrane with a spoon. Place butternut squash, cut sides down, in a 13 x 9–inch baking dish coated with cooking spray. Pierce squash multiple times with a fork. Bake at 400° for 45 minutes or until squash is very tender. Cool squash 10 minutes. **3. Remove** cooked squash from skins using a spoon, and place in a food processor. Process until smooth, adding 1 tablespoon water, if needed, to reach desired consistency. **Yield:** 1½ cups or 6 (¼-cup) servings.

kitchen tip

Large squash can be difficult to cut. To make cutting easier and safer, pierce the squash several times with a sharp knife. Microwave it at HIGH 1 minute: cut it in half as directed in recipe.

vegetable purees

Once baby tolerates the First Purees well, try introducing other vegetables and fruits. Baby will love the new colors and flavors.

Green Beans ❊

Green beans are very fibrous, which makes it hard to get a smooth consistency. Straining after pureeing will help remove any stringy pieces. Try using frozen green beans if fresh are not in season.

1   pound green beans, trimmed

1. Place green beans in a vegetable steamer. Steam, covered, 15 minutes or until very tender. Remove beans from steamer, reserving cooking liquid. **2. Place** beans in a food processor; process until smooth, adding cooking liquid, 1 tablespoon at a time, to reach desired consistency. Strain using a sieve or food mill, if needed; discard solids. **Yield:** 1½ cups or 6 (¼-cup) servings.

❊ *Denotes recipes that freeze well.*

---

maintaining nutrients

You may notice that most of the purees call for steaming rather than boiling. That's because the less water the vegetable or fruit comes in contact with, the more vitamins and minerals the food retains. Some nutrients still leach into the water when you steam, which is why we recommend saving and using the cooking liquid to help smooth and thin your purees.

Sweet Potatoes ❊

Baking the sweet potato caramelizes the natural sugars in the potato giving it a rich, sweet flavor. You can also steam the cubed peeled sweet potato in a steamer basket for 20 to 25 minutes or until very tender.

2   large sweet potatoes (about 13 ounces each)
2   tablespoons water, formula, or breast milk

1. Preheat oven to 400°. **2. Pierce** each potato several times with a fork. Bake at 400° for 55 minutes to 1 hour or until tender. Cool 45 minutes or until cool enough to handle. **3. Peel** sweet potatoes. Place flesh in a food processor; process until smooth, adding 2 tablespoons water, formula, or breast milk, 1 tablespoon at a time, to reach desired consistency. **Yield:** 2½ cups or 10 (¼-cup) servings.

Broccoli

Both the broccoli stalk and florets are a great source of vitamins for baby. In some babies, broccoli can contribute to gas. If this happens, wait a few weeks, and then reintroduce broccoli.

1   (1¾-pound) bunch broccoli

1. Cut broccoli stalk into 1-inch pieces; separate head into small florets. Place stalk and florets in a vegetable steamer. Steam, covered, 14 minutes or until very tender. Remove broccoli from steamer, reserving cooking liquid. **2. Place** broccoli in a food processor; process until smooth, adding cooking liquid, 1 tablespoon at a time, to reach desired consistency. Strain using a sieve or food mill, if needed; discard solids. **Yield:** 1¾ cups or 7 (¼-cup) servings.

Beets ❋

The bright-red color of beets is appealing to babies, but be careful since this vegetable easily stains clothes. If you notice that subsequent diapers take on a reddish tint, don't be alarmed; it's normal for babies who eat beets.

2   beets (about 11 ounces)

1. Preheat oven to 400°. **2. Leave** root and 1-inch stem on beets; scrub with a brush. Wrap each beet in foil. Bake at 400° for 1 hour or until tender. Remove from oven; cool slightly. Trim off beet root; rub off skin. Cut beets in half. Place in a food processor; process until smooth, adding water, 1 tablespoon at a time, if needed, to reach desired consistency. **Yield:** 2 cups or 8 (¼-cup) servings.

Yellow Squash

Summer squash have a high water content, so you usually don't need to add extra liquid to thin the purees. The higher water content, though, means yellow squash and zucchini don't freeze as well as other purees.

4 yellow squash (about 1¼ pounds), cut into ¼-inch-thick slices

1. **Place** squash in a vegetable steamer. Steam, covered, 7 minutes or until very tender. 2. **Place** squash in a food processor; process until smooth. **Yield:** 2 cups or 8 (¼-cup) servings.

Zucchini

3 zucchini (about 1 pound), cut into ¼-inch-thick slices

1. **Place** zucchini in a vegetable steamer. Steam, covered, 8 minutes or until very tender. 2. **Place** zucchini in a food processor; process until smooth. **Yield:** 2 cups or 8 (¼-cup) servings.

Asparagus ✳

This nutrient-rich vegetable is a great green to introduce. It's common for baby's urine to take on a strong odor after eating asparagus, so don't be alarmed.

1 pound asparagus, trimmed and cut into 1½-inch pieces

1. **Place** asparagus in a vegetable steamer. Steam, covered, 9 minutes or until very tender. Remove asparagus from steamer, reserving cooking liquid. 2. **Place** asparagus in a food processor; process until smooth, adding cooking liquid, 1 tablespoon at a time, to reach desired consistency. Strain using a sieve or food mill, if needed; discard solids. **Yield:** 1¼ cups or 5 (¼-cup) servings.

✳ *Denotes recipes that freeze well.*

at our house
Drama queen

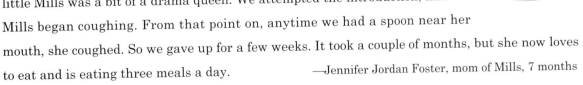

When Mills was 4 months old, our pediatrician suggested we begin introducing her to food. He said to give her a few bites every day. Well, my husband and I quickly learned that our little Mills was a bit of a drama queen. We attempted the introduction, and Mills began coughing. From that point on, anytime we had a spoon near her mouth, she coughed. So we gave up for a few weeks. It took a couple of months, but she now loves to eat and is eating three meals a day.

—Jennifer Jordan Foster, mom of Mills, 7 months

fruit purees

Babies love the naturally sweet flavors of fruit. Once introduced, fruit makes great additions to cereal and vegetable purees.

~~~~~~

Apples ✳

Choose Gala, Golden Delicious, Rome, or Pink Lady apples for this puree. They are sweeter and less acidic than other apples such as Granny Smiths.

4   apples (about 2 pounds), peeled, cored, and quartered

1. Place apples in a vegetable steamer. Steam, covered, 12 minutes or until very tender. **2. Place** apples in a food processor; process until smooth. **Yield:** 2 cups or 8 (¼-cup) servings.

Pears ✳

Be sure to peel and cut the pears just before you cook them so they won't have time to turn brown.

4   ripe pears, peeled, cored, and quartered

1. Place pear in a vegetable steamer. Steam, covered, 8 minutes or until tender. **2. Place** pear in a food processor; process until smooth. **Yield:** 1 ½ cups or 6 (¼-cup) servings.

✳ *Denotes recipes that freeze well.*

Plums ✳

This sweet and juicy fruit is a great staple to mix with other purees when you start expanding baby's menu.

6   plums, peeled, halved, and pitted

1. Place plums in a vegetable steamer. Steam, covered, 7 minutes or until very tender. **2. Place** plums in a food processor; process until smooth. **Yield:** 1½ cups or 6 (¼-cup) servings.

kitchen tip

The riper the fruit, the less steaming time it takes to soften the flesh, so use the lower end of the cook time range.

Peaches

Very ripe peaches that are soft, sweet, and juicy don't need to be steamed, and you may be able to puree them with just a fork or potato masher.

4   ripe peaches (about 1½ pounds), peeled, halved, and pitted

1. Place peaches in a vegetable steamer. Steam, covered, 6 minutes or until tender. **2. Place** peaches in a food processor; process until smooth. **Yield:** 1½ cups or 6 (¼-cup) servings.

Apple Puree

Dried Plums ✳

Dried plums or prunes are the one fruit we recommend boiling because they need direct contact with water to help fully rehydrate the fruit.

⅔ cup dried pitted plums (about 14)
2½ cups water

1. Place dried plums and water in a saucepan; bring to a boil. Cover, reduce heat, and simmer, 10 minutes or until dried plums are very tender. **2. Remove** dried plums from saucepan, reserving cooking liquid. Place plums in a food processor; process until smooth, adding cooking liquid, 1 tablespoon at a time, to reach desired consistency. Strain dried plum mixture through a sieve into a small bowl; discard solids. **Yield:** 1 cup or 4 (¼-cup) servings.

Kiwifruit

Babies love the bright green color of kiwis. Since kiwifruit is so soft and easy to puree, it's a great fruit to serve when you're in a hurry or on the go. Kiwifruit can be slightly acidic, so try stirring it into pureed banana the first time you feed it to baby.

1 kiwifruit, peeled and quartered

1. Place kiwifruit in a small bowl; mash with a fork until smooth, or place in a small food processor, and process until smooth. **Yield:** about ⅓ cup or 1 (⅓-cup) serving.

✳ *Denotes recipes that freeze well.*

Cantaloupe

This is a great summer dish to serve when cantaloupes are at their peak in freshness. Because of the high water content of cantaloupes, we don't recommend freezing this puree.

1 cantaloupe (about 2½ pounds), peeled, seeded, and cut into chunks

1. Place cantaloupe in a vegetable steamer. Steam, covered, 3 minutes or until tender. **2. Place** cantaloupe in a food processor; process until smooth. **Yield:** 2 cups or 8 (¼-cup) servings.

Mango

Very tender, ripe mangos might be soft enough to mash and serve to baby without having to steam them.

2 peeled ripe mango, cut into 4 wedges (about 1¾ pound

1. Place mango wedges in a vegetable steamer. Steam, covered, 8 minutes or until very tender. **2. Place** mango in a food processor; process until smooth. Strain using a sieve or food mill; discard solids. **Yield:** 1½ cups or 6 (¼-cup) servings.

cooking liquid

Fruits puree well because of their high water content. For most of these purees, you usually won't need to add more water, but we've suggested you save the cooking liquid until you puree the fruit just in case you need to thin it.

Papayas

Introduce baby to the tropics with this fruit that's high in vitamin C. While very ripe papayas can be mashed with a fork, you'll usually have better results when you steam them before pureeing.

1 ripe papaya (about 1 pound), peeled, halved, and seeded

1. Place papaya in a vegetable steamer. Steam, covered, 8 minutes or until very tender. **2. Place** papaya in a food processor; process until smooth. **Yield:** 1 cup or 4 (¼-cup) servings.

at our house

Eating socially

Dinner is our family's favorite meal of the day. There is an indescribable joy in watching Audrey taste foods for the first time. When she was 4 months old, we introduced fruits and vegetables to her diet. Initially her lips were pursed together so tightly you couldn't slide a slip of paper into her little mouth. We were afraid that she would never enjoy eating with a spoon. As a joint effort, we sent her food to day care, and she quickly became a social eater. Even as babies, they prefer to eat in groups. Now at 7 months, she makes the cutest and most perfect oval to accept her food. She's also experimenting with finger foods, putting both of her teeth to good use. There is such gratification on her face and ours when food makes it into her mouth instead of her nose. Cheering and clapping at our table is now a dinnertime ritual.

—Amorice Law, mom of Audrey, 7 months

first combinations

After introducing your baby to fruits and vegetables, you can begin serving mixtures. With so many fruits and vegetables to choose from, the possibilities for tasty combinations are endless.

No-Cook Tropical Fruits

The natural acidity in the papaya will help prevent this banana mixture from beginning to turn brown immediately. This puree does not freeze well, so plan to serve it within 1 to 2 days.

2 kiwifruit, peeled and quartered
1 papaya, peeled, seeded, and chopped
1 ripe banana, peeled and cut into ½-inch-thick slices

1. Place fruit in a food processor; process until smooth. **Yield:** 2 cups or 8 (¼-cup) servings.

Apples, Pears, and Plums ✳

This fruit blend is a favorite alone or stirred into rice cereal.

2 ripe pears, peeled, cored, and quartered
1 large Golden Delicious apple, peeled, cored, and quartered
2 plums, peeled, halved, and pitted

1. Place pear and apple in a vegetable steamer. Steam, covered, 8 minutes.

combinations

As baby's palate expands, get creative with puree combinations. You can try any combination you wish, but here are some of our favorites:

- Rice cereal and any fruit puree
- Rice cereal and any vegetable puree
- Squash and peach
- Avocado and banana
- Beet and carrot
- Prune and banana
- Sweet potato and apricot
- Papaya and mango
- Squash and zucchini
- Asparagus and zucchini
- Pear and prune
- Sweet potato and peach

Add plums; cover and steam an additional 4 minutes or until all fruit is tender. **2. Place** fruit in a food processor; process until smooth. **Yield:** 2 cups or 8 (¼-cup) servings.

Garden Vegetables ✳

Vegetable medleys are a favorite with babies. Don't have one of the vegetables called for? Substitute any vegetable that baby has already tried.

1 cup fresh or frozen petite green peas, thawed
1 cup green beans, trimmed, or broccoli florets
3 carrots (about ½ pound), cut into ¼-inch-thick slices

1. Arrange all vegetables in a vegetable steamer. Steam, covered, 13 minutes or until vegetables are very tender. Remove vegetables from steamer, reserving cooking liquid. **2. Place** vegetables in a food processor; process until smooth, adding cooking liquid, 1 tablespoon at a time, to reach desired consistency. **Yield:** 2 cups or 8 (¼-cup) servings.

Many grocery stores now sell canned organic pumpkin, sweet potato, and butternut squash. These are great options for baby when you don't have time to cook since they usually only require a little breast milk or formula and stirring to loosen the texture to that of a baby puree. Choose a brand that lists only the vegetable and water in the ingredient list.

Apples and Butternut Squash ✳

Butternut squash is easiest to find during the fall and winter months, but it will keep for several weeks when stored uncut in a cool, dry place. Choose a squash that is hard, smooth, and blemish free.

1 butternut squash (about 1 pound)
Cooking spray
3 Golden Delicious apples, peeled, cored, and quartered

1. Preheat oven to 400°. **2. Cut** squash in half lengthwise; remove seeds and membrane with a spoon. Place butternut squash, cut sides down, in a 13 x 9–inch baking dish coated with cooking spray. Pierce squash multiple times with a fork. Bake squash at 400° for 15 minutes; add apples to dish. Bake an additional 30 minutes or until apples and squash are very tender. **3. Let** apples and squash cool 10 minutes. Remove cooked squash from shells, and place in a food processor; add apples. Process until smooth. **Yield:** 3 cups or 12 (¼-cup) servings.

✳ *Denotes recipes that freeze well.*

Spinach and Sweet Potatoes ✳

Packed full of vitamins A and C, this tasty puree can easily be doubled.

1 large sweet potato (about 10 ounces)
2 cups bagged baby spinach leaves

1. Preheat oven to 400°. **2. Pierce** sweet potato several times with a fork. Bake at 400° for 45 minutes or until tender. Cool 45 minutes or until cool enough to handle. Peel sweet potato, and place flesh in a food processor. **3. While** potato bakes, place spinach in a vegetable steamer. Steam, covered, 3 minutes or until spinach wilts. Reserve cooking liquid. **4. Add** spinach to potato in food processor; process until smooth, adding cooking liquid, 1 tablespoon at a time, to reach desired consistency. **Yield:** 1 cup or 4 (¼-cup) servings.

Spinach and Sweet Potatoes

8 to 12 months

Exploring New Textures and Tastes

You've survived those first feedings and the
messes they bring. Now that you're feeling
more confident about feeding baby, it's time
to enjoy the last few months of your little
one's first year by exploring new tastes and
textures.

new foods for a new stage

Baby is growing and is now ready to experience even more new tastes, textures, and food combinations. As baby's food options expand, both meal preparation and mealtime will become more enjoyable for the whole family.

Progressing to three meals

Around the age of 8 months, you should begin to think about offering solids more than once or twice per day. Most babies at this age have grown to love mealtime, and their improved mouth control (and increasing number of teeth) make it easier for them to chew. Slowly, solids foods will become a larger part of baby's diet and nutrition. Plan meals that contain a variety of proteins, grains and starches, and fruits and vegetables. But don't stress: Each meal doesn't have to have a food from each group. Instead, focus on providing a variety of foods from each group over the course of a day.

Protein

We don't have to tell you that baby is busy now, and protein is important for giving her the energy to keep crawling, rolling, playing, and babbling. Starting at 6 months, babies need protein foods that are rich in iron and zinc, and it should begin to come from solid food sources. In other words, breast milk or formula isn't enough to sustain your little one's needs now.

Protein-rich foods include meats (beef and pork), poultry (chicken and turkey), dairy foods (yogurt and cheese), eggs, beans, and tofu. Introduce these foods just like you've done before—as simple purees or strained mixtures. Once baby has tried several, begin offering two or three different types of proteins during the day at either meals or snacks.

Our Sample Feeding Chart on page 43 shows offering different proteins at lunch (beans or cheese), for a mid-afternoon snack (cottage cheese or yogurt), and at dinner (meat, poultry, or tofu). Of course, these are just our suggestions—do whatever works best for your baby and your schedule. Combined with baby's milk, these foods will provide plenty of protein for baby at this stage of her development.

Whole grains

During this stage, baby also can try tasty grain and starch foods like rice and pasta. You can grind or chop these foods, or, if baby is ready, offer them as very soft bite-sized pieces. Try to offer whole-grain varieties (such as whole-wheat pasta and brown rice) as much as possible, since they provide more fiber, protein, vitamins, and minerals than their refined counterparts.

Combination foods

In addition, this is a good time to begin offering more combination foods that mix protein, a starch or grain, and a fruit or vegetable. Baby will like the new taste combinations, and you will like the convenience of one-dish meals. Combining foods is also a great way to sneak in a healthy food that baby may not eat by itself. Incorporate foods for baby that the whole family is already eating—and you're already cooking.

sample feeding chart for baby who eats three meals a day

The amounts in this sample feeding chart are just estimates, so make adjustments based on your baby's needs. As your little one eats more solid meals over the next few months, you may notice that his milk consumption decreases. This is normal and completely healthy as long as baby gets between 16 and 28 ounces of milk per day.

Breakfast	Mid-morning	Lunch	Mid-afternoon	Dinner	Bedtime
• ¼ to ½ cup cereal or oatmeal mixed with ¼ cup applesauce • 4 to 6 oz. baby's milk	• ¼ to ½ cup pears or other fruit or vegetable • Teething toast or soft whole-grain cracker	• ¼ to ½ cup green beans or other green vegetable • ¼ cup mashed beans or ¼ to ½ cup cheese • 4 to 6 oz. baby's milk	• ¼ to ½ cup cottage cheese or yogurt • ¼ to ½ cup plums or other fruit • 4 to 6 oz. baby's milk	• ¼ cup meat, poultry, or tofu • ¼ to ½ cup butternut squash or other orange or yellow vegetable • ¼ cup brown rice • 4 to 6 oz. baby's milk	• 6 to 8 oz. baby's milk

Growing independence

You might have noticed that you're living with a miniature copycat. Your baby likes to (try to) do whatever he sees you do. Between 8 and 10 months, he will bring this attitude to the table and begin showing an interest in feeding himself by grasping for the spoon or trying to pick up food.

Let baby start to feed himself by offering finger foods and letting him try to use a spoon, or at least hold one. Beginner finger foods should be very soft, tender, and bite-sized. Try things like soft fruits (such as bananas), steamed vegetables, shredded meats, dry cereal (such as whole-grain toasted Os), and crackers that dissolve in baby's mouth (such as teething toasts and graham crackers).

As baby experiments with using his fingers and utensils, mealtimes may temporarily begin to be more about learning and motor development, rather than eating—and that's OK. However, you should still feed baby some of the food until he is proficient at getting food into his mouth.

The American Academy of Pediatrics also recommends giving baby a cup at this age. You can try a "sippy" cup with a lid and soft or hard spout, or a small nonbreakable cup. Again, this initially will be more of a learning experience, so baby may not drink much from the cup at first. Continue to offer the cup at mealtimes, and soon your baby will prefer the cup.

Exploring New Textures and Tastes **43**

what about juice?

Over the past few years, juice has become somewhat of a controversial beverage choice for children, in part because of the rise in childhood obesity. Juice labeled 100-percent fruit juice, however, is a good source of vitamin C and technically does count toward daily fruit servings. So is juice healthy or harmful to baby?

Here's the lowdown: 100-percent fruit juice offers no nutritional benefit to your child that fruit itself can't provide. In fact, juice doesn't provide as many vitamins or fiber as fruit provides and can have extra calories. Other juice concerns are that baby will begin to prefer juice over healthier beverages like milk or water and that baby will fill up on juice instead of eating nutritious meals and snacks.

Cinnamon-Apple Yogurt

Pear, plum, or apple purees are taste sub-stitutions for apple. As baby gets older and begins enjoying different textures, you can mash soft, ripe fruits and add them to yogurt instead of the purees.

2   servings of Apple Puree (page 34) or ½ cup natural applesauce
1   cup plain yogurt
Dash of cinnamon

1. Stir Apple Puree or apple-sauce into yogurt. Serve imme-diately, or cover and refrigerate. **Yield:** 1½ cups or 3 (½-cup) servings.

freezing purees

In the previous chapter, we suggested that your life would be easier when you prepared foods in bulk and refrigerated or froze baby's purees. As baby's food options expand, there will be more foods you can simply stir together just before serving, and they may not necessarily freeze well. We've kept the yields smaller on these recipes so you will have ample time to refrigerate and serve all that the recipe prepares. Foods in this chapter that can be prepared in bulk and frozen will have slightly larger yields and a "freezes well" notation. ❄

Cottage Cheese and Fruit

Select a cottage cheese made with whole or 2% milk; babies need the extra fat now for proper growth and development. Also, baby may tolerate the texture of small curds better than large-curd varieties. We do not recommend freez-ing this recipe.

½   cup cottage cheese
1   serving of Pear Puree (page 34) or ¼ cup peeled, mashed ripe pear
1   serving of Peach Puree (page 34) or ¼ cup peeled mashed peaches

1. Combine all ingredients in a small bowl, stirring well. For a smoother texture, place all ingredients in a food proces-sor, and process until desired consistency. **Yield:** 1 cup or 2 (½-cup) servings.

Basic Oatmeal with Fruit

Add a frozen fruit puree cube to a bowl of hot oatmeal to cool it down quickly and add extra nutrients. You can also prepare the oatmeal in the microwave; combine the oats and water in a microwave-safe bowl, and microwave at HIGH 1 minute. Stir in mashed banana, and make sure the oatmeal has cooled before serving.

¼ cup old-fashioned or quick-cooking oats
½ cup water
½ ripe banana, mashed

1. Place oats in a food processor or blender; process 30 seconds or until a powder consistency. **2. Bring** water to a boil in a small saucepan. Stir in oats. Reduce heat to low, and cook, uncovered, 3 to 4 minutes or until smooth, stirring occasionally. **3. Stir** in mashed banana. **Yield:** about ¾ cup or 1 (¾-cup) serving.

Oatmeal with Fruit and Yogurt variation: Stir 2 tablespoons plain yogurt into oatmeal and fruit mixture.

Blueberry-Banana Yogurt

This stir-together dish is chunkier and thicker in texture than some babies like. To make it smoother, try pureeing the blueberries and banana, rather than mashing them by hand, and adding a tablespoon of baby's milk.

¼ cup blueberries
½ ripe banana
½ cup plain yogurt

1. Place blueberries and banana in a small bowl; mash with a fork until well blended and few chunks remain. Stir into yogurt. Serve immediately, or cover and refrigerate. **Yield:** 1 cup or 2 (½-cup) servings.

Basic Oatmeal with Fruit

Cheesy Broccoli Potatoes

Swiss cheese has a slightly sweet flavor that babies often like, but mild cheddar, cottage cheese, or mozzarella make good substitutes. Be sure to choose Swiss cheese labeled "baby Swiss" instead of "aged Swiss," which can have a very strong flavor.

1   large baking potato, peeled and cut into
      1-inch cubes
⅔   cup broccoli florets
⅓   cup (1½ ounces) shredded Swiss cheese

1. Place potato in a saucepan; cover with water. Bring to a boil. Reduce heat, and simmer 10 minutes. Add broccoli; cook an additional 7 minutes or until potato and broccoli are tender. **2. Drain** potato and broccoli; place in a small bowl. Add cheese, and let stand until cheese melts. **3. For** a chunkier texture, mash potato mixture with a potato masher to desired consistency. For a smoother texture, place potato mixture in a food processor, and process until desired consistency. **Yield:** 1¾ cups or about 3 (½-cup) servings.

portion sizes

Baby's eating more now, so serving sizes have increased to about ½ cup for most of the recipes in this chapter. Feel free to adjust and make servings smaller or larger based on your baby's needs and appetite. If you're unsure how much your baby will eat, portion out a small amount in a bowl for baby, and place the remainder in a storage container. If baby wants more, use a clean spoon to add more to baby's bowl; if not, cover and refrigerate or freeze the remainder.

Brown Rice and Carrots

Be sure to try the avocado variation—whole grains mixed with avocado's good-for-you fat and the antioxidants found in carrots provide a one-dish dinner full of nutrients. We do not recommend freezing or reheating avocado, so stir it in just before serving.

¾ cup uncooked long-grain brown rice

3 large carrots, peeled and cut into ¼-inch-thick slices (about ¾ pound)

1. Prepare rice according to package directions, omitting salt and fat. **2. Place** carrot in a vegetable steamer. Steam, covered, 15 minutes or until very tender. Remove carrot from steamer, reserving cooking liquid. **3. Place** carrot in a food processor, and process 30 seconds. Add rice, and process until desired consistency, adding cooking liquid, 1 tablespoon at a time, if needed. **Yield:** 1½ cups or 3 (½-cup) servings.

Brown Rice with Carrots and Mashed Avocado variation: Stir 2 to 3 tablespoons of mashed avocado into the brown rice–and–carrot mixture just before serving it.

---

at our house

A dislike of peas

Well, I thought I was going to have very similar food experiences with Eli as I did with his older brother. I knew that I had to provide him with various food choices to see what foods he preferred, as well as for allergy purposes. Of course, I started slowly, and I discovered that there weren't many foods Eli did NOT like! In fact, he actually liked sitting at the table, and he watched intently as we ate as a family. By the time I had taken Eli through the fruits and some of the vegetables, it was time to introduce him to a vegetable his brother loved as a baby—peas. Eli, however, showed great dislike for peas. I had to come up with some way to have him at least taste the food for the reasons I mentioned above, and I decided that the best way to present peas to him was by mixing a small amount with a fruit I knew he liked. To my amazement, not only did Eli eat them, but he wanted more! Lately, I have found that I am mixing foods quite a bit to get Eli to eat some things better and make mealtimes easier and quicker, which is a plus for a busy mom.

—Jennifer Boackle Dunn, mom of Eli, 8 months, and Sam, 4 years

Lentils and Sweet Potatoes

Lentils come in many varieties—red, green, and brown, to name a few. All have a mild flavor and are good sources of protein and fiber. Combining this puree with rice provides baby with all the essential amino acids.

1½	cups water
½	cup apple juice
¼	teaspoon ground cinnamon
1	cup dried lentils
¾	cup Sweet Potato Puree (page 30 or canned mashed sweet potato

1. Combine first 3 ingredients in a medium saucepan; bring to a boil. Add lentils; cook 35 minutes or until lentils are very tender. Drain; let cool completely.
2. Place lentils in a food processor; process until smooth. Stir in Sweet Potato Puree. **Yield:** 2¾ cups or about 5 (½-cup) servings.

beans

Beans are healthy, inexpensive, and easy to prepare, making them a great option for baby. They're an excellent source of protein and complex carbohydrates, not to mention that they're full of fiber. Because of this mix of nutrients, both toddlers and adults feel satisfied longer after a meal with beans.

Most beans can be purchased dried or canned. Dried have no added sodium or preservatives, but they take a little more time to prepare; they must be soaked in water overnight, or for several hours, and then cooked. Canned versions are much more convenient, but they're higher in sodium; you can reduce the sodium in canned beans by rinsing and draining them several times. Although you should limit your baby's sodium intake as much as possible, you don't need to worry about canned beans too much—the amount of sodium in a small baby-sized serving isn't harmful.

Most babies love all types of beans. You can serve them mashed or whole as finger foods; however, cut larger beans in half if you are serving them as finger foods. Here are a few to try:

- Black beans
- Small red beans
- Lentils
- Black-eyed peas
- Butter beans
- Great Northern beans
- Green peas
- Edamame

Lentil Pilaf with Sweet Potatoes variation: Stir ¾ cup cooked brown or long-grain rice into lentils before processing. Proceed with the recipe as directed. **Yield:** 3½ cups or 7(½-cup) servings.

Basic Chicken Dinner ❋

Cooked chicken breasts can be difficult to puree to a consistency that baby will like. We've found that using ground chicken is a much easier option. You can substitute ground turkey for the ground chicken, if you'd like.

Cooking spray
½ pound ground chicken
¼ teaspoon dried rubbed sage
1 cup cooked brown rice
Water, breast milk, or formula

1. Heat a medium skillet over medium heat; coat pan with cooking spray. Add chicken; cook 8 minutes or until browned, stirring to crumble. Stir in sage. **2. Place** chicken mixture and rice in a food processor; process until desired consistency, adding water, breast milk, or formula, 1 tablespoon at a time, if needed. **Yield:** 2 cups or 4 (½-cup) servings.

Chicken and Rice with Apples variation: Stir 3 servings of Apple Puree (page 34) or 1 cup peeled, steamed apple slices into processed chicken and rice mixture. Add water, breast milk or formula, 1 tablespoon at a time, if needed, until desired consistency. **Yield:** 2½ cups or 5 (½-cup) servings.

Chicken, Spinach, and Rice variation: Place 3 cups bagged baby spinach leaves in a vegetable steamer. Steam, covered, 3 minutes or until spinach wilts. Add steamed spinach to processed chicken and rice mixture; process until desired consistency, adding cooking liquid, 1 tablespoon at a time, if needed. **Yield:** 2 cups or 4 (½-cup) servings.

Basic Beef Dinner ❋

Beef is a great source of iron, zinc, and B vitamins—all essential nutrients that little bodies need to grow healthy and strong. You can easily double this recipe and store the leftovers in the freezer for up to one month.

1 small butternut squash (about 1 pound)
Cooking spray
½ pound ground round

1. Preheat oven to 400°. **2. Pierce** squash several times with the tip of a sharp knife. Microwave at HIGH 1 minute. Cut squash in half lengthwise; remove seeds and membrane with a spoon. Place squash, cut sides down, on a foil-lined baking sheet. Pierce squash multiple times with a fork. Bake at 400° for 45 minutes or until squash is very tender. Cool squash 10 minutes.

3. While squash bakes, heat a medium nonstick skillet over medium-high heat; coat pan with cooking spray. Add ground round; cook 4 minutes or until browned, stirring to crumble. Drain and place in a food processor. **4. Remove** cooked squash from skins, and place in food processor with ground round. Process until desired consistency. **Yield:** 1½ cups or 3 (½-cup) servings.

Beef and Veggies Variation: Stir 2 servings Green Beans (page 30) into Basic Beef Dinner or add ½ cup cooked green beans to squash and beef in food processor before processing. **Yield:** 2 cups or 4 (½-cup) servings.

❋ *Denotes recipes that freeze well.*

Fruit fan

We started Georgia on solids after her 4-month checkup. She had always been a great eater, so I was looking forward to filling her stomach with something besides milk. We started with cereal, and she loved it. When I introduced some vegetables, the whole process came to screeching halt. She would have nothing to do with vegetables—absolutely nothing at all. So I tried some fruit, and she ate more that day than ever before. She loved fruit so much that it was the only thing she ate until she began on table food at 10 months. I could have freaked out—and some people even told me that I was ruining her taste buds by allowing her to get used to the sweet taste, but I knew that stage would pass. And it has. Now, at 18 months, I have a super, well-rounded eater. Sure, she prefers sweets, but it has nothing to do with eating only fruit for 6 months. It comes straight from her momma.

—Heather Goss, mom of Georgia, 16 months

fish and mercury

Fish is a great source of lean protein, omega-3 fatty acids, and vitamin B_{12}. Even though fish contains many nutrients, some are high in mercury and should be avoided. According to the Food and Drug Administration, fish is a safe option for children if you follow these guidelines:

- Avoid shark, swordfish, king mackerel, and tilefish.
- Choose fish lowest in mercury like catfish, cod, flounder, haddock, perch, pollock, salmon, scallops, shrimp, sole, tilapia, trout, canned light tuna, and whitefish.
- Limit servings to two to three times per week.

Basic Fish Dinner ❄

Choose fish that have firm, shiny flesh, and make sure all the bones have been removed before processing it and serving to baby.

1   large baking potato (about 14 ounces), peeled and cut into 1-inch cubes
½   pound flounder or other mild white fish
3   tablespoons water

1. **Place** potato in a saucepan; cover with water. Bring to a boil. Reduce heat; simmer 15 minutes or until tender; drain, reserving cooking liquid. Let potato cool slightly. 2. **While** potato cooks, place fish in a microwave-safe dish; add 3 tablespoons water to dish. Cover with heavy-duty plastic wrap; vent. Microwave at HIGH 3 to 4 minutes or until fish flakes easily when tested with a fork. Let fish cool slightly; flake with a fork, and remove and discard bones, if needed. 3. **Place** fish, potato, and 3 table-

teething toasts

The word *zwieback* is German and means "twice baked," which perfectly describes these crunchy teething toasts that will likely become a favorite of baby's to hold and chew. These toasts are not designed for baby to bite and eat, but rather to gum and practice using their new teeth. Stale biscuits and crackers may also be used as teething toasts; just be sure they will dissolve slowly when chewed on and don't break into pieces that baby could cause baby to choke.

While they don't provide much added nutritional benefit, teething toasts can assist baby in practicing his motor skills related to eating and be a great diversion for the baby who likes to grab at the feeding spoon. Make sure your baby has already started solids and is able to grab objects and chew on them before introducing teething toasts. Some babies are ready for teething toasts as early as 6 months, while others may not be ready until 8 to 10 months. If in doubt, check with your pediatrician.

Zwieback Toasts

Making your own teething toast for baby lets you choose whole-grain bread and avoid added preservatives. It also saves money—a loaf of bakery whole-grain bread averages around $3, while the equivalent amount of packed toasts costs anywhere from $7 to $9.

1   (1-pound) loaf whole-wheat bread, cut into
     ½-inch slices

1. Preheat oven to 250°. **2. Cut** each slice of bread lengthwise into thirds, and place on an ungreased baking sheet. Bake at 250° for 1 hour or until bread is crisp. Let cool completely before serving. Store in an airtight container. **Yield:** 42 slices.

spoons reserved cooking liquid in a food processor. Process until desired consistency, adding additional cooking liquid, 1 tablespoon at a time, if needed. **Yield:** 3 cups or 6 (½-cup) servings.

Fish Dinner with Veggies variation: Stir 1 serving each of Green Peas (page 29) and Carrots (page 28) purees into Basic Fish Dinner. **Yield:** 3½ cups or 7 (½-cup) servings.

Cheesy Fish and Potatoes variation: Sprinkle ½ cup (2 ounces) shredded mild cheddar cheese over drained potato. Let cheese melt while potato cools. Follow above procedure for Steps 2 and 3. **Yield:** 3 cups or 6 (½-cup) servings.

❄ *Denotes recipes that freeze well.*

the next step at mealtime

During the last few months of baby's first year, start thinking about how you can modify dishes that you are already preparing for the rest of the family for baby to eat as well. The benefits: you have less to prepare for dinner, and baby loves eating what everyone else is enjoying. The recipes on these pages have instructions for how you can use the same ingredients to also make a meal for baby. This is just the start of incorporating baby into your family mealtimes!

Become a Baby Food Chef

Once baby has tasted a variety of foods, experiment with combinations to create your own baby dinner. Make mealtime easier by combining the key ingredients that you are already using for the rest of the family's meal. Depending on baby's age, puree, finely chop, or cut the food into small finger food pieces.

¼ cup protein
    (lean ground beef, skinless boneless chicken breast, lean ground turkey, or fish cooked thoroughly, cooled, and chopped, or silken tofu, drained and chopped)

¼ cup cooked starch
    (cooked brown rice, beans, whole-wheat pasta, couscous, or potato or sweet potato cubes)

¼ cup steamed vegetables
    (carrot slices, peas, green beans, broccoli florets, spinach, squash, or zucchini) OR 1 serving of a fruit or vegetable puree in chapter 2, Weaning Baby

1. Place protein, starch, and vegetable in a food processor; process until desired consistency, adding water or other liquid, 1 tablespoon at a time, if needed. **Yield:** about ⅔ cup or 1 (⅔-cup) serving.

Southwestern Salad Bar

The whole family will have fun putting together their own salads. This lineup has some-thing for everyone—even baby!

for baby: To prepare **Southwestern Chicken Dinner** for baby, place ¼ cup chopped cooked chicken, ¼ cup cubed peeled avocado, ¼ cup chopped peeled mango, and 1 tablespoon water in a food processor; process until desired consistency. **Yield:** about ½ cup.

for baby: To prepare **Southwestern Bean Mash** for baby, place ¼ cup drained canned black beans, ¼ cup cubed peeled avocado, ¼ cup chopped peeled mango, and 1 tablespoon water in a food processor. Process until desired consistency. **Yield:** about ½ cup.

kitchen tip

Baby's version can be served as small finger foods instead of processed once he's ready for it.

1	tablespoon fajita seasoning
2	cups fresh corn kernels (about 4 ears)
5	teaspoons fresh lime juice, divided
2	teaspoons minced fresh cilantro
⅔	cup chopped red onion
2	garlic cloves, minced
2	(15-ounce) cans black beans, rinsed and drained
1	(7-ounce) bottle roasted red bell peppers, drained and chopped
½	cup diced peeled avocado
¾	cup light ranch dressing
1½	teaspoons minced canned chipotle chiles in adobo sauce
12	cups packaged chopped romaine lettuce
3	cups chopped skinless, boneless rotisserie chicken
1½	cups (6 ounces) preshredded reduced-fat Mexican blend or cheddar cheese
1½	cups unsalted baked tortilla chips, crumbled (about 2½ ounces)
1	cup mango, peeled and chopped
1	cup sliced green onions
½	cup thinly sliced radishes

1. Cook seasoning in a large saucepan over medium heat 2 minutes or until toasted, stirring frequently. Combine fajita season-ing, corn, 1 tablespoon juice, and cilantro in a medium serving bowl. **2. Combine** onion and next 3 ingre-dients in a medium serving bowl. Combine avocado and remaining 2 teaspoons juice in a small serv-ing bowl, tossing gently to coat. Combine dressing and chipotle in a small serving bowl. **3. Place** lettuce in a large serving bowl. Place chicken in a medium serving bowl. Place cheese, chips, mango, green onions, and radishes in individual serving bowls. Arrange bowls buffet-style, beginning with lettuce and ending with dressing. For each serving: 1½ cups lettuce, ¾ cup bean mixture, ¼ cup corn mixture, about ⅓ cup chicken, 3 tablespoons chips, 3 tablespoons cheese, 2 tablespoons mango, 2 tablespoons onions, 1 tablespoon radishes, 1 tablespoon avocado, and 1½ tablespoons dressing. **Yield:** 8 adult servings.

CALORIES 411; FAT 12.7g (sat 2.5g, mono 4.6g, poly 4.2g); PROTEIN 32g; CARB 45.9g; FIBER 11.3g; CHOL 55mg; IRON 3.7mg; SODIUM 822mg; CALC 179mg

Spinach and Butternut Squash Lasagna

This recipe has several steps, but the end result is worth the extra effort. Try making it on a weekend, and enjoy leftovers on a busy weeknight.

for baby: For **Baby's First Lasagna,** prior to lasagna assembly in Step 7, set aside ¼ cup cooked squash, 2 tablespoons cooked spinach, and one-third of 1 cooked lasagna noodle. Place all in a food processor; sprinkle with 1 teaspoon grated Parmigiano-Reggiano cheese. Process until desired consistency, adding breast milk or formula, 1 tablespoon at a time, if needed. **Yield:** about ½ cup. **NOTE:** For babies age 11 to 12 months, a small portion of prepared lasagna can be scooped out and pureed. It's recommended you decrease the salt and pepper in recipe; adults can add them at the table if needed.

3   cups 2% reduced-fat milk
1.1 ounces all-purpose flour (about ¼ cup)
2   tablespoons butter
⅓   cup minced shallots
¾   teaspoon salt, divided
½   teaspoon freshly ground black pepper, divided
5½   cups (¾-inch) cubed peeled butternut squash (about 2½ pounds)
1   tablespoon balsamic vinegar
4   teaspoons olive oil, divided
Cooking spray
1   teaspoon chopped fresh thyme
4   garlic cloves, minced
3   (6-ounce) packages fresh baby spinach
9   cooked lasagna noodles
1   cup (4 ounces) shredded Asiago cheese
1   cup (4 ounces) grated fresh Parmigiano-Reggiano cheese

1. Heat milk in a small, heavy saucepan over medium-high heat to 180° or until tiny bubbles form around edge (do not boil). Remove from heat; keep warm. **2. Weigh** or lightly spoon flour into a dry measuring cup; level with a knife. Melt butter in a medium nonstick saucepan over medium heat. Add shallots; cook 2 minutes or until tender. Reduce heat; add flour to pan, and cook 5 minutes or until smooth and golden, stirring constantly. Remove from heat; add about 2 tablespoons warm milk to flour mixture, stirring constantly with a whisk. Gradually add remaining warm milk, about ½ cup at a time, until mixture is smooth, stirring constantly with a whisk. Stir in ½ teaspoon salt and ¼ teaspoon black pepper. Bring to a boil; reduce heat, and cook until smooth and thickened. Remove from heat. Cover surface of milk mixture with plastic wrap; set aside. **3. Preheat** oven to 425°. **4. Place** squash in a large bowl. Add vinegar; toss to

coat. Add 1 tablespoon oil; toss to coat. Arrange squash in a single layer on a jelly-roll pan coated with cooking spray; sprinkle with remaining ¼ teaspoon pepper and thyme. Bake at 425° for 30 minutes, stirring after 15 minutes. **5. Combine** remaining 1 teaspoon oil and garlic in a Dutch oven over medium heat; cook 2 minutes, stirring constantly. Add spinach, 1 bag at a time; cook until wilted, stirring frequently. Add remaining ¼ teaspoon salt; cook until liquid evaporates, stirring frequently. **6. Reduce** oven temperature to 350°. **7. Spoon** ⅓ cup milk mixture in bottom of a 13 x 9-inch baking pan coated with cooking spray. Arrange 3 noodles over milk mixture; top with spinach mixture, ⅔ cup milk mixture, ½ cup Asiago, and ¼ cup Parmigiano-Reggiano. Arrange 3 noodles over cheese; top with squash mixture, ⅔ cup milk mixture, remaining ½ cup Asiago, and ¼ cup Parmigiano-Reggiano. Arrange remaining 3 noodles on top of cheese; spread remaining ½ cup milk mixture over noodles. Sprinkle with remaining ½ cup Parmigiano-Reggiano. Bake at 350° for 30 minutes or until bubbly. Let stand 15 minutes before serving. **Yield:** 8 adult servings.

CALORIES 445; FAT 15g (sat 8.1g, mono 4.2g, poly 0.7g); PROTEIN 20.7g; CARB 61.5g; FIBER 7.3g; CHOL 36mg; IRON 4.8mg; SODIUM 758mg; CALC 599mg

Baby's First Lasagna

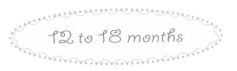

12 to 18 months

Expanding Meals

Mealtimes are fun for both babies and parents during this stage. Babies are better at feeding themselves now, and they are still eager to try almost any food you put in front of them.

eating together

During this stage, parents can have fun exposing young palates to new foods and flavors and watching the reactions of their little ones. Mealtime also gets a lot easier since babies can begin eating versions of what you serve the rest of the family. Little ones love trying what mom, dad, and older siblings are eating, and parents appreciate the simplicity of fixing just one meal for everyone.

All by myself

Babies at this age will eat almost anything—as long as they get to feed themselves. These are signs of maturity (both socially and developmentally) and baby's budding independence, all of which are healthy and should be encouraged. During the early part of this stage, babies will usually use their fingers to eat since they're still developing the dexterity to eat with a utensil. Offer utensils, but don't be surprised if your little one prefers to use his or her fingers. Toward the end of this stage, baby will begin using utensils more.

Nutrition changes

During this stage, you may notice that baby's appetite decreases slightly. This is completely normal as baby's rate of growth slows after the first year. Be sure you offer your little one nutrient-rich options so that when she does eat, it's good for her. Meals and snacks should incorporate a variety of grains and starches, fruits and vegetables, proteins, and dairy foods. Cow's milk should be baby's primary beverage, but it can be supplemented with water and occasionally juice.

Toddler-friendly dishes and utensils

Help baby feed himself by stocking up on toddler-friendly dishes and utensils. Bowls and dishes should be small and nonbreakable. Smaller dishes are less intimidating to babies, so they usually prefer food served on smaller plates. The plates should have a rim to help scoop up bites. Divided rimmed plates can help prevent baby from having to chase a bite across the plate with a utensil. Spoons and forks should be shorter than adult versions and have thick, chunky handles to help baby grasp them.

Exposing baby to new flavors

Babies develop food preferences early, so part of your job as a parent is to expand your child's palate by exposing her to as many healthy foods as possible. Since baby is receptive to new foods at this age, it's an ideal window to offer offer a variety of textures and flavors. This can mean incorporating herbs and mild spices into your cooking, combining unusual food textures (such as finely chopped nuts in a rice pilaf), or simply offering fruits and vegetables your toddler has yet to try.

Pulling baby up to the table

If you haven't already made the transition, pull your toddler's high chair or booster seat up to the family table, and let baby eat with the rest of the family at mealtimes. He will enjoy the social interaction and more importantly see his parents and siblings eating the same healthy foods he is eating. Referred to as "modeling," this concept is important because what toddlers see others eating impacts what they unconsciously decide to eat for the rest of their lives.

Feeding baby the family meal

Feeding your toddler what the rest of the family is eating is often a tougher hurdle for parents to get over than it actually is for baby. But remember, your child is ready and technically has been eating more tender, plainer versions of adult food for a while now. It's important not to label food as "adult food" or "kid food" because it creates connotations for your toddler of what he should or shouldn't eat. Your little one will try almost all foods right now, so this is a perfect age to offer dishes and foods the rest of the family is eating. Plus, it simplifies mealtime tremendously for the cook!

at our house

Adventurous eating

Micah loves to eat! Of course, sweets are his absolute favorite, but he enjoys any flavor and texture placed before him. I didn't purposely create an adventurous eater, but he certainly is! Until he was 12 months old, I was a typical first-time mommy. I stuck to the basics for fear of the dreaded allergic reaction, but shortly after Micah turned 1, I began to relax. His first adventurous tasting occurred while we were at a local sandwich shop with a friend. I have never liked black olives, but I thought I'd see if Micah would share the sentiment. Oh, how surprised I was as he chewed and swallowed his first bite. He grinned and then took another bite! I've since introduced Micah to everything from hummus to avocado and stewed tomatoes. The only food he's ever turned his nose up at was plain yogurt. I'm proud of my little man, and I'm making an effort to encourage his bold eating manner by introducing him to a new food almost weekly.

—Alisa Martin, mom of Micah, 15 months

transitional recipes

The recipes in this chapter are designed to help you transition baby to the family meal. Each recipe is a family-friendly recipe, and next to each one you'll find directions on how to modify or adapt a small serving of that recipe for baby. Get excited because this is the beginning of simplified meal planning!

~~~~~~

Mini Whole-Wheat Apricot Muffins

To ensure that the apricots are soft enough for baby, soak them in hot water for 10 minutes; drain them well before chopping them.

for baby: Serve 1 to 2 cooled mini muffins.

2.25 ounces all-purpose flour (about ½ cup)
1.6 ounces whole-wheat flour (about ⅓ cup)
¼ cup sugar
¾ teaspoon grated orange rind
½ teaspoon baking soda
⅛ teaspoon salt
½ cup low-fat buttermilk
2 tablespoons butter, melted
¼ teaspoon vanilla extract
1 large egg white
½ cup finely chopped dried apricots
Cooking spray

1. Preheat oven to 375°. **2. Weigh** or lightly spoon flours into dry measuring cups; level with a knife. Combine flours, sugar, and next 3 ingredients in a large bowl; make a well in center of mixture. **3. Combine** buttermilk and next 3 ingredients in a bowl; stir with a whisk. Add buttermilk mixture to flour mixture; stir just until moist. Fold in apricots. Spoon batter into 24 mini muffin cups coated with cooking spray. Bake at 375° for 10 minutes or until muffins spring back when touched lightly in center. Remove from pans immediately; cool on a wire rack. **Yield:** 8 adult servings (serving size: 3 mini muffins).

CALORIES 133; FAT 3.2g (sat 1.9g, mono 0.8g, poly 0.2g); PROTEIN 3g; CARB 23.6g; FIBER 1.4g; CHOL 8mg; IRON 1mg; SODIUM 159mg; CALC 27mg

smart snacking

five reasons we love muffins for toddlers

- Perfect for quick breakfasts—and great for snacks too!
- Portable, ideal for school lunch boxes, car rides, and diaper bags.
- Easy to keep on hand because most freeze well. (Store them in airtight, freezer-safe containers, pull them out as needed, and defrost them in the microwave.)
- A great way to sneak in extra fruit, vegetables, whole grains, and fiber.
- Requires no assistance from mom or dad—toddlers can feed themselves.

Mini Whole-Wheat Apricot Muffins

Blueberry Oatmeal Muffins

Introduce baby to this family favorite made even more healthy by adding whole-wheat flour and oatmeal. Tossing unthawed frozen blueberries with a couple tablespoons of flour before adding them to the batter keeps them from turning the batter purple while they bake. If you use fresh blueberries, skip that step.

for baby: **Serve ½ to 1 cooled muffin.**

1⅔   cups quick-cooking oats
3   ounces all-purpose flour (about ⅔ cup)
2.33 ounces whole-wheat flour (about ½ cup)
¾   cup packed light brown sugar
2   teaspoons ground cinnamon
1   teaspoon baking powder
1   teaspoon baking soda
¾   teaspoon salt
1½   cups low-fat buttermilk
¼   cup canola oil
2   teaspoons grated lemon rind
2   large eggs
2   cups frozen blueberries
2   tablespoons all-purpose flour
Cooking spray
2   tablespoons granulated sugar

1. Preheat oven to 400°. **2. Place** oats in a food processor; pulse 5 to 6 times until oats resemble coarse meal. Place in a large bowl. **3. Weigh** or lightly spoon flours into dry measuring cups; level with a knife. Add flours and next 5 ingredients to oats in bowl; stir well with a whisk. Make a well in center of mixture. **4. Combine** buttermilk and next 3 ingredients in small bowl; stir well with a whisk. Add to flour mixture, stirring just until moist. **5. Toss** berries with 2 tablespoons flour, and gently fold into batter. Spoon batter into 16 muffin cups coated with cooking spray; sprinkle 2 tablespoons granulated sugar evenly over batter. Bake at 400° for 20 minutes or until muffins spring back when touched lightly in center. Remove from pans immediately; place on a wire rack. Serve warm or at room temperature. **Yield:** 16 adult servings (serving size: 1 muffin).

CALORIES 190; FAT 5g (sat 0.6g, mono 2.4g, poly 1.2g); PROTEIN 4.2g; CARB 33.3g; FIBER 2.4g; CHOL 23mg; IRON 1.6mg; SODIUM 248mg; CALC 74mg

---

smart snacking

snacking for energy

Babies at this age typically eat two to three snacks per day partly due to their small stomach sizes, which don't allow them to eat like adults do at meals. Try pairing a carbohydrate food with a protein food to keep baby full of energy.

Healthy Carbohydrate Options:
- Whole-grain toasted oat cereal
- Whole-grain cheddar fish snacks
- Banana slices or other cut up fruit
- Mini rice cakes
- Raisins or other tender dried fruit
- Whole-grain crackers

Healthy Protein Options:
- Soft cheese cubes or slices
- Yogurt
- Deli meat cubes or slices
- Cottage cheese
- Hard-boiled egg slices
- Peanut butter or almond butter

Oatmeal Raisin Muffins

Look for untoasted wheat germ in the organic food section of your supermarket. Adding boiling water to the batter and allowing it to sit for 15 minutes before baking allows the hearty oats, wheat germ, and bran to soak up the liquid for a more tender muffin.

for baby: Serve ½ to 1 cooled muffin.

4.75 ounces whole-wheat flour (about 1 cup)
¼   cup granulated sugar
¼   cup packed brown sugar
2   tablespoons untoasted wheat germ
2   tablespoons wheat bran
1½ teaspoons baking soda
1   teaspoon ground cinnamon
½   teaspoon salt
1½ cups quick-cooking oats
⅓   cup chopped pitted dates
⅓   cup raisins
⅓   cup dried cranberries
1   cup low-fat buttermilk
¼   cup canola oil
1   teaspoon vanilla extract
1   large egg, lightly beaten
½   cup boiling water
Cooking spray

1. Weigh or lightly spoon flour into a dry measuring cup; level with a knife. Combine flour and next 7 ingredients in a large bowl, stirring with a whisk. Stir in oats and next 3 ingredients. Make a well in center of mixture. Combine buttermilk and next 3 ingredients; add to flour mixture, stirring just until moist. Stir in boiling water. Let batter stand 15 minutes. **2. Preheat** oven to 375°. **3. Spoon** batter into 12 muffin cups coated with cooking spray. Bake at 375° for 20 minutes or until muffins spring back when touched lightly in center.

Remove muffins from pans immediately; place on a wire rack. **Yield:** 12 adult servings (serving size: 1 muffin).

CALORIES 204; FAT 6.4g (sat 0.8g, mono 3.2g, poly 1.8g); PROTEIN 4.6g; CARB 34.7g; FIBER 3.4g; CHOL 19mg; IRON 1.4mg; SODIUM 288mg; CALC 43mg.

Mini Ham-and-Cheese Frittatas

Both little and big kids will enjoy these cheesy egg bites. Store leftover frittatas in the refrigerator for up to 5 days or freeze for up to 1 month.

for baby: Serve a cooled frittata in a small bowl or on a rimmed plate.

2   cups finely chopped peeled baking potato (about 2 medium)
2   teaspoons canola oil
¼   teaspoon salt
½   cup (3 ounces) diced extralean ham
¼   cup (1 ounce) shredded mild cheddar cheese
7   large egg whites, lightly beaten
3   large eggs, lightly beaten
Cooking spray

1. Preheat oven to 375°. **2. Place** potato in a saucepan; cover with water. Cover and bring to a boil. Reduce heat; simmer 7 minutes or until almost tender. Drain. **3. Heat** oil in a large nonstick skillet over medium-high heat. Add potato and salt; cook 7 minutes or until potato is lightly browned. **4. Combine** potato, ham, and next 3 ingredients in a large bowl. Spoon mixture into 16 muffin cups coated with cooking spray. Bake at 375° for 15 minutes or until lightly browned. Cool in pans on a wire rack 5 minutes; remove from pans. **Yield:** 8 adult servings (serving size: 2 frittatas).

CALORIES 118; FAT 4.4g (sat 1.6g, mono 1.7g, poly 0.7g); PROTEIN 9.3g; CARB 9.3g; FIBER 0.6g; CHOL 79mg; IRON 0.6mg; SODIUM 178mg; CALC 42mg

Whole-Wheat Buttermilk Pancakes

Serve the pancakes with heated maple syrup. Remember that serving sizes are designed for adult needs; baby will eat less and need only a small drizzle of syrup.

for baby:

- Cut a pancake into bite-sized pieces and serve on a rimmed plate.
- Drizzle lightly with syrup.

3.4 ounces all-purpose flour (about ¾ cup)
6.3 ounces whole-wheat flour (about ¾ cup)
3 tablespoons sugar
1½ teaspoons baking powder
½ teaspoon baking soda
½ teaspoon salt
1½ cups low-fat buttermilk
1 tablespoon vegetable oil
1 large egg
1 large egg white
Cooking spray
¾ cup maple syrup
3 tablespoons butter

1. **Weigh** or lightly spoon flours into dry measuring cups; level with a knife. Combine flours and next 4 ingredients in a large bowl, stirring with a whisk. Combine buttermilk and next 3 ingredients, stirring with a whisk. Add to flour mixture, stirring just until moist.

2. **Heat** a nonstick griddle or nonstick skillet coated with cooking spray over medium heat. Spoon about ¼ cup batter per pancake onto griddle. Turn pancakes over when tops are covered with bubbles and edges look cooked. Serve with syrup and butter. **Yield:** 6 adult servings (serving size: 2 pancakes, 2 tablespoons syrup, and 1½ teaspoons butter).

CALORIES 351; FAT 10g (sat 4.6g, mono 2.8g, poly 1.9g); PROTEIN 7.6g; CARB 59.7g; FIBER: 2.3g; CHOL 55mg; IRON 2.1mg; SODIUM 570mg; CALC 176mg

kitchen tip

Keep cooked pancakes warm in a 200° oven while preparing remaining pancakes, and then serve to the whole family.

Breakfast Couscous

Couscous are tiny granules of semolina flour that cook up light and fluffy in just a few minutes. This is a great time-saving recipe for busy mornings because you can prepare it the night before and reheat it in the morning. The recipe is easy to double if you need to serve more people.

for baby:

- Serve cooled spoonfuls in a small bowl.
- Omit walnuts, if desired.

¼ cup water
1 cup 1% low-fat milk
½ cup uncooked couscous
¼ cup dried cranberries or other small dried fruit
¼ cup raisins
¼ cup chopped walnuts, toasted
2 tablespoons brown sugar
½ teaspoon ground cinnamon
⅛ teaspoon salt

1. **Bring** water to a boil in a small saucepan; stir in milk and remaining ingredients. Remove from heat. Cover; let stand 10 minutes. (Mixture will thicken as it cools.) **Yield:** 3 adult servings (serving size: ⅔ cup).

CALORIES 314; FAT 7.6g (sat 1.2g, mono 1.2g, poly 4.8g); PROTEIN 8.3g; CARB 56g; FIBER 3.4g; CHOL 3mg; IRON 1.3mg; SODIUM 147mg; CALC 137mg

A not-so-picky eater

When John Paul first began to eat table foods, I had completely prepared myself for a battle in regard to him being a picky eater. After all, his mom is an extremely picky eater so he will most likely follow suit, right? Well, wrong. Instead of battling with him about eating enough, I had to figure out how to keep him from eating too much. There was nothing he would not eat, except for peas (which he eventually developed a taste for). I asked the pediatrician numerous times, "Can I feed him too much?" to which he replied, "No." So I continued feeding my little boy a variety of foods. The battle ensued when mealtime was over. My lovable, smiling little boy who loved mealtime so much turned into a tantrum-toting, head-flinging terror at the end of any meal. Finally, I realized that little bits of food (such as puffed cereal) at the end of the meal served as a perfect transition food. So now as mealtime comes to an end, I simply pull out the puffs and begin the wind-down process. Does it work every time to ward off a tantrum? No, but I'll take it 75 percent of the time!

—Lauryn Schultz, mom of John Paul, 12 months

Rise and Shine Oatmeal

Oatmeal is a great way for both parents and baby to start the day. This whole grain has complex carbs, protein, and fiber, which help supply a steady stream of energy to the body. Using milk in place of water to make the oatmeal gives the hot cereal an extra boost of calcium. For additional flavor, sprinkle it with chopped walnuts and brown sugar.

for baby: Serve cooled spoonfuls in a small bowl.

2   cups 1% low-fat milk
2   cups old-fashioned oats
½   cup golden raisins
2   tablespoons honey
½   teaspoon salt
½   teaspoon vanilla extract
½   teaspoon ground cinnamon

1. Bring milk to a boil over medium heat. Stir in oats; cook 5 minutes. Remove from heat; stir in raisins and remaining ingredients. **Yield:** 4 adult servings (serving size: 1 cup).

CALORIES 296; FAT 4.4g (sat 1.2g, mono 1.2g, poly 0.9g); PROTEIN 10.2g; CARB 58.5g; FIBER 4.7g; CHOL 5mg; IRON 2.5mg; SODIUM 357mg; CALC 184mg

Mac and Cheese with Roasted Tomatoes

Introduce baby to this comfort food classic that the whole family will love as a main dish or side. Plenty of milk and cheese make it a great source of bone-building calcium. Feel free to use a mild cheddar, if you'd like.

for baby:

- Omit black pepper.
- Serve spoonfuls in a small bowl.
- Cut the tomatoes and macaroni, if needed, into bite-sized pieces.

Cooking spray

8	plum tomatoes (about 2 pounds), cut into ¼-inch-thick slices
1	tablespoon olive oil
1	tablespoon minced fresh thyme
¾	teaspoon salt, divided
4	garlic cloves, thinly sliced
1	pound uncooked multigrain whole-wheat elbow macaroni
2.25	ounces all-purpose flour (about ½ cup)
5	cups 1% low-fat milk
1½	cups (6 ounces) shredded extrasharp white cheddar cheese
1	cup (4 ounces) shredded fontina cheese
½	teaspoon black pepper
½	cup (2 ounces) grated fresh Parmesan cheese
⅓	cup dry breadcrumbs

1. Preheat oven to 400°. **2. Cover** a baking sheet with aluminum foil, and coat foil with cooking spray. Arrange tomato slices in a single layer on baking sheet. Drizzle oil over tomatoes. Sprinkle with thyme, ¼ teaspoon salt, and garlic. Bake at 400° for 35 minutes or until tomatoes start to dry out. **3. Cook** pasta according to package directions, omitting salt and fat. Drain well. **4. Place** flour in a large Dutch oven; gradually add milk, stirring with a whisk until blended. Cook over medium heat 8 minutes or until thick and bubbly, stirring constantly with a whisk. Add cheddar, fontina, remaining ½ teaspoon salt, and pepper, stirring until cheese melts. Remove from heat. Stir in tomatoes and pasta. Spoon into a 13 x 9-inch baking dish coated with cooking spray. Combine grated Parmesan cheese and breadcrumbs; sprinkle over pasta mixture. Bake at 400° for 25 minutes or until bubbly. **Yield:** 10 adult servings (serving size: about 1 cup).

CALORIES 411; FAT 14g (sat 6.9g, mono 2.9g, poly 0.9g); PROTEIN 22.8g; CARB 49.9g; FIBER: 4.7g; CHOL 39mg; IRON 2.5mg; SODIUM 638mg; CALC 414mg

nutrition note

why milk matters

First birthdays mark the time to start offering whole cow's milk to baby. Although adults may think of whole milk as a rich, high-fat beverage, that's exactly what baby needs at this age. In fact, the extra fat that whole milk provides is essential for baby's development. Occasionally, pediatricians may recommend 2% milk for babies with strong family histories of heart disease, obesity, and high cholesterol. Check with your child's pediatrician to be sure, but for most babies, whole milk is the most nutritious choice.

After their second birthday, toddlers can be slowly weaned to low-fat or skim milk. Cow's milk should remain baby's staple beverage for adequate amounts of calcium, vitamin A, vitamin D, and protein.

If your baby has a cow's milk allergy, soy milk is a good alternative. It's important, however, to understand that soy milk provides no additional health benefit to baby. In fact, soy milk can be deficient in key vitamins and minerals. If baby is older than 1 and needs soy instead of cow's milk, be sure to choose full-fat soy milk, as well as one that is fortified with calcium and vitamins A and D.

Mac and Cheese with Roasted Tomatoes

Even though baby is eating foods the rest of the family is eating, remember that baby needs far less than the amount you serve to bigger kids or yourself. So how do you know exactly how much to put on baby's plate? One rule of thumb suggests that baby should be given about one-fourth of an adult serving. Since serving sizes can vary, another way to look at this is about 1 to 2 tablespoons of each food, with slightly more of the starch or grain.

Below are some starting points for serving sizes for baby. Remember that each baby is different, and his or her appetite will change. Your little one may eat more or less, so watch and adapt servings to meet his or her needs.

Fruits	about 1 to 2 tablespoons
Vegetables	about 1 to 2 tablespoons
Grains or starch	about 3 to 4 tablespoons
Protein	about ½ to 1 ounce

Barley with Shiitakes and Spinach

Although barley isn't a commonly used grain, it's great for baby because of its mild flavor. In this recipe, barley provides a quick yet hearty base for vegetables, cheese, and rosemary, which can be served as a meatless main or side dish.

for baby:
- Omit black pepper.
- Serve the barley mixture in a small bowl.
- Cut the mushrooms and spinach into bite-sized pieces, if needed.

2	teaspoons olive oil
1	cup chopped onion
½	teaspoon chopped dried rosemary
3	garlic cloves, minced
8	cups sliced shiitake mushroom caps (about 1¼ pounds)
¾	cup uncooked quick-cooking barley
1	(14-ounce) can fat-free, less-sodium beef broth
8	cups bagged baby spinach leaves
3	tablespoons shredded Parmesan cheese
¼	teaspoon freshly ground black pepper

1. Heat oil in a Dutch oven over medium-high heat. Add onion, rosemary, and garlic; sauté 3 minutes. Add mushrooms; cook 8 minutes or until vegetables are tender, stirring occasionally. **2. Stir** in barley and broth. Bring to a boil; cover, reduce heat, and simmer 15 minutes or until barley is tender. **3. Add** spinach, cheese, and pepper; cover and cook 2 minutes or until spinach wilts, stirring frequently. **Yield:** 6 adult servings (serving size: about 1 cup).

CALORIES 148; FAT 2.7g (sat 0.8g, mono 1.1g, poly 0.2g); PROTEIN 6.8g; CARB 23.5g; FIBER 4.2g; CHOL 3mg; IRON 2.9mg; SODIUM 225mg; CALC 78mg

Barley with Shiitakes and Spinach

Pan-Grilled Snapper with Orzo Pasta Salad

Small rice-shaped pasta, orzo cooks quickly and soaks up flavor from the vinaigrette. Double the vinaigrette, and spoon some over the top of the fish, if you like.

for baby:
- Omit black pepper.
- Shred the fish into bite-sized pieces.
- Serve fish and a spoonful of orzo mixture in a small bowl or on a rimmed plate.

1½ cups uncooked orzo (rice-shaped pasta)
Cooking spray
4 (6-ounce) red snapper fillets
½ teaspoon salt, divided
¼ teaspoon black pepper, divided
1½ tablespoons minced shallots
1 tablespoon chopped fresh parsley
1 tablespoon fresh lemon juice
2 teaspoons orange juice
1 teaspoon Dijon mustard
2½ tablespoons extra-virgin olive oil

1. Cook pasta according to package directions, omitting salt and fat. Drain and keep warm. **2. Heat** a grill pan over medium-high heat; coat pan with cooking spray. Sprinkle fish evenly with ¼ teaspoon salt and ⅛ teaspoon pepper. Add fish to pan; cook 3 minutes on each side or until fish flakes easily when tested with a fork. **3. Combine** remaining ¼ teaspoon salt, remaining ⅛ teaspoon pepper, shallots, and next 4 ingredients in a small bowl, stirring well. Slowly add oil, stirring constantly with a whisk. Drizzle shallot mixture over pasta; toss well to coat. **Yield:** 4 adult servings (serving size: 1 fillet and ¾ cup pasta mixture).

CALORIES 398; FAT 11.2g (sat 1.8g, mono 6.9g, poly 1.6g); PROTEIN 32.7g; CARB 39.3g; FIBER 1.9g; CHOL 47mg; IRON 0.4mg; SODIUM 409mg; CALC 46mg

Pilaf with Chicken, Spinach, and Walnuts

You'll need a large skillet with a lid for this recipe. Breaking the cinnamon sticks and sautéing them with the onion brings out their aromatic goodness. To save time, use chicken breast meat from a rotisserie chicken.

for baby:
- Omit the walnuts and dill.
- Serve spoonfuls in a small bowl.

1½ tablespoons olive oil, divided
1 cup chopped onion
2 (3-inch) cinnamon sticks, broken
1½ cups uncooked basmati rice
1 cup diced plum tomato
½ teaspoon salt
2 (14-ounce) cans fat-free, less-sodium chicken broth
1 (6-ounce) package fresh baby spinach, coarsely chopped
½ cup raisins
2 cups chopped cooked chicken breast (about 2 breasts)
½ cup coarsely chopped walnuts, toasted
2 tablespoons finely chopped fresh dill

1. Heat 1 tablespoon oil in a large nonstick skillet over medium-high heat. Add onion and cinnamon sticks; sauté 5 minutes or until lightly browned. Stir in rice, and sauté 1 minute. Stir in remaining 1½ teaspoons oil, tomato, salt, and broth. Bring to a boil; cover, reduce heat, and simmer 15 minutes or until rice is tender and liquid is absorbed. **2. Add** spinach and raisins; sauté 2 minutes or until spinach wilts. Discard cinnamon sticks. Stir in chicken. Sprinkle with walnuts and dill. **Yield:** 6 adult servings (serving size: 1⅔ cups).

CALORIES 393; FAT 12.1g (sat 1.6g, mono 3.9g, poly 5.4g); PROTEIN 21.3g; CARB 52.7g; FIBER 4.6g; CHOL 40mg; IRON 7.1mg; SODIUM 977mg; CALC 62mg

kitchen tip

At this age, baby enjoys feeding himself, often with his fingers. Offer him utensils, but don't be surprised if he prefers his fingers. Baby will eventually begin using utensils more.

71

Spaghetti with Turkey-Veggie Meatballs

For younger tots try serving with a whole-grain pasta that's easy to pick up, such as penne, rigatoni, or fusilli. *or egg noodles*

for baby:

- Crumble a meatball.
- Cut a spoonful of spaghetti into small pieces.
- Combine the meatball crumbles, spaghetti, and 1 to 2 tablespoons of sauce in a small bowl.

1	large egg white *(use whole egg)*
¼	teaspoon salt
¼	teaspoon pepper
2	garlic cloves, minced
1½	pounds ground turkey *(use pork and beef)*
½	cup dry breadcrumbs
½	cup (2 ounces) finely shredded Parmesan cheese
⅓	cup finely chopped green onions *(¼ c onion)*
¼	cup coarsely shredded carrot
¼	cup coarsely shredded zucchini
¼	cup chopped fresh parsley
	Cooking spray
1	(24-ounce) jar tomato-basil pasta sauce (such as Classico)
6	cups cooked multigrain or whole-wheat spaghetti (about 7 ounces uncooked)

1. Preheat oven to 400°. **2. Combine** egg white and next 3 ingredients in a large bowl, stirring with a whisk. Add turkey and next 6 ingredients; combine using hands. With moist hands, shape mixture into 32 (1½-inch) balls. Place meatballs on a broiler pan coated with cooking spray. Bake at 400° for 15 minutes or until done. **3. Heat** pasta sauce in a large saucepan over medium heat until hot. Add meatballs, stirring to coat. Serve meatballs and sauce over pasta. **Yield:** 6 adult servings (serving size: 1 cup pasta, about 5 meatballs, and about ½ cup sauce).

CALORIES 408; FAT 12.5g (sat 4.1g, mono 0.1g, poly 0.2g); PROTEIN 35.5g; CARB 42.6g; FIBER 7.2g; CHOL 78mg; IRON 3.3mg; SODIUM 799mg; CALC 248mg

kitchen tip

Use a small ice-cream scoop to divide the meat mixture for perfectly portioned meatballs.

Beef and Vegetable Potpie

Cooking the beef filling first in a large skillet and then in the oven ensures that the meat and vegetables are tender and flavorful. Finishing the casserole in the oven browns the breadstick-dough topping. For a fun presentation kids will love, make individual servings in 4-ounce ramekins. You can also freeze single servings for later.

for baby: Serve spoonfuls of potpie in a small bowl.

1	tablespoon olive oil, divided
1	pound ground sirloin
2	cups chopped zucchini
1	cup chopped onion
1	cup chopped carrot
1	teaspoon dried basil
½	teaspoon dried thyme
1	(8-ounce) package presliced mushrooms
3	garlic cloves, minced
¼	cup tomato paste
1½	teaspoons Worcestershire sauce
½	teaspoon freshly ground black pepper
1	(14-ounce) can fat-free, less-sodium beef broth
2	tablespoons cornstarch
2	tablespoons water
	Cooking spray
1	(11-ounce) can refrigerated soft breadstick dough

1. **Preheat** oven to 400°. 2. **Heat** 1½ teaspoons oil in a large nonstick skillet over medium-high heat. Add beef; cook 3 minutes or until browned, stirring to crumble. Drain. Wipe drippings from pan with a paper towel. Heat remaining 1½ teaspoons oil in pan. Add zucchini and next 6 ingredients; sauté 7 minutes or until vegetables are tender. Return beef to pan. Stir in tomato paste and next 3 ingredients. Bring to a boil; cook 3 minutes. Combine cornstarch and 2 tablespoons water in a small bowl; stir with a whisk. Add cornstarch mixture to pan; cook 1 minute, stirring constantly. 3. **Spoon** beef mixture into an 11 x 7-inch baking dish coated with cooking spray. Separate breadstick dough into strips. Arrange strips in a lattice fashion over beef mixture. Bake at 400° for 12 minutes or until browned. **Yield:** 6 adult servings (serving size: 1⅓ cups).

CALORIES 313; FAT 8.5g (sat 1.7g, mono 3g, poly 0.7g); PROTEIN 22 g; CARB 37.6g; FIBER 2.7g; CHOL 40mg; IRON 3.9mg; SODIUM 679mg; CALC 41mg

Herbed Pork Tenderloin with Creamy Polenta

Fresh herbs provide flavor that won't overwhelm baby. Marinate the pork the day before, and then, you only have a quick 30-minute dinner to prepare the next day.

for baby:
• Omit black pepper in the pork and polenta.
• Shred a small amount of the cooked pork.
• Serve shredded pork and polenta in a small bowl or on a rimmed plate.

Pork:
1 tablespoon chopped fresh rosemary
1 tablespoon chopped fresh thyme
1 tablespoon chopped fresh marjoram
1 tablespoon chopped fresh oregano
1 tablespoon extra-virgin olive oil
½ teaspoon salt
¼ teaspoon freshly ground black pepper
4 garlic cloves, minced
2 (1-pound) pork tenderloins, trimmed
Cooking spray

Polenta:
½ cup finely chopped onion
2 garlic cloves, minced
½ cup low-sodium chicken broth
5 cups water, divided
1 cup dry polenta
1 tablespoon butter
1 teaspoon salt
¼ teaspoon freshly ground black pepper

1. **To prepare** pork, combine first 9 ingredients in a large zip-top plastic bag; seal and marinate in refrigerator overnight or for up to 2 days. 2. **Preheat** oven to 400°. 3. **Remove** pork from bag. Place pork on a broiler pan coated with cooking spray. Bake at 400° for 30 minutes or until a thermometer registers 155°. Remove from oven; cover and let stand 10 minutes before slicing. 4. **To prepare** polenta, heat a medium saucepan over medium-high heat. Coat pan with cooking spray. Add onion and 2 garlic cloves; sauté 2 minutes. Add broth; cook 5 minutes or until liquid almost evaporates. Add 2½ cups water; reduce heat, and simmer 5 minutes. Gradually add polenta, stirring constantly with a whisk. Cook over medium heat 15 minutes or until thick and creamy, stirring frequently and gradually adding remaining 2½ cups water. Stir in butter, 1 teaspoon salt, and ¼ teaspoon pepper. Serve with pork. **Yield:** 8 adult servings (serving size: about 3 ounces pork and about ¾ cup polenta).

CALORIES 221; FAT 7.1g (sat 2.3g, mono 3.6g, poly 0.7g); PROTEIN 25.3g; CARB 13g; FIBER 1.6g; CHOL 77mg; IRON 2mg; SODIUM 511mg; CALC 23mg

Peas and Pods

Round, sweet, and perfect for little fingers, peas are a hit with babies. Mint adds bright flavor and accents the natural sweetness of the peas.

for baby:
- Serve spoonfuls in a small bowl or on a rimmed plate.
- Cut the sugar snap peas into bite-sized pieces.
- Omit mint, if desired.

¾   pound sugar snap peas, trimmed
2   cups fresh or frozen petite green peas, thawed
1½   tablespoons butter, softened
¼   teaspoon kosher salt
2   tablespoons finely chopped fresh mint

1. Steam snap peas, covered, 2 minutes. Add green peas to pan; steam 2 minutes. **2. Combine** peas, butter, and salt in a large bowl; toss gently to coat. Sprinkle with mint. **Yield:** 6 adult servings (serving size: ⅔ cup).

CALORIES 87; FAT 2.8g (sat 1.8g, mono 0.7g, poly 0.1g); PROTEIN 3.4g; CARB 10.7g; FIBER 3.4g; CHOL 7.5mg; IRON 1.3mg; SODIUM 105mg; CALC 42mg

nutrition note

peas

Peas are bursting with nutrients. They're packed with protein and fiber plus an assortment of vitamins and minerals, including vitamins C and A and folate.

Edamame Mashed Potatoes

Edamame are fresh young soybeans. In this recipe, they add fiber and protein to ordinary mashed potatoes as well as a fun green color.

for baby:
- Serve spoonfuls in a small bowl or on a rimmed plate.

1½   cups frozen shelled edamame (green soybeans)
2½   cups cubed peeled baking potato (about 1 pound)
1   cup fat-free, less-sodium chicken broth
½   cup water
½   cup 2% reduced-fat milk
1   tablespoons olive oil
¾   teaspoon salt
Dash of ground white pepper

1. Cook edamame in boiling water 10 minutes or until tender. Drain and set aside. **2. Place** potato, chicken broth, and water in a large saucepan. Cover and bring to a boil. Reduce heat, and simmer 12 minutes or until tender. Drain, reserving ½ cup cooking liquid. **3. Place** edamame in a food processor; process until finely chopped. With processor on, slowly pour reserved cooking liquid through food chute, processing until smooth. **4. Place** edamame mixture, potato, milk, and remaining ingredients in a large bowl. Mash with a potato masher to desired consistency. **Yield:** 4 adult servings (serving size: about ¾ cup).

CALORIES 230; FAT 7.1g (sat 1.1g, mono 2.7g, poly 0.5g); PROTEIN 11g; CARB 31.1g; FIBER 4.7g; CHOL 3mg; IRON 2.5mg; SODIUM 570mg; CALC 70mg

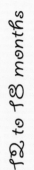

nutrition notes

food and mood

Are there particular times of day when your toddler is testier than others? Most likely it's late morning and late afternoon, and this may be due to a slight drop in blood sugar. Two to three hours after a meal, babies at this age run out of fuel, and blood sugar levels start to fall. Toddlers may quickly become irritable—just as some adults do when they go too long between meals. To avoid imminent meltdowns, keep these simple tips in mind:

• **Plan Well:** Make sure your child gets a good source of protein at each meal. When eaten with complex carbohydrates, protein keeps you full longer and helps keep blood sugars stable.

• **Snack Smart:** Toddlers' stomachs are small and need fuel in between meals. Offer your child a snack about two to three hours after the last meal. Try pairing a protein-rich food with carbohydrate-rich food (see Snacking for Energy on page 62).

• **Be Prepared:** If you are going to be away from home during baby's normal snack or mealtime, pack nutritious snacks to take with you. Keep a snack supply in your car or diaper bag for "emergencies."

Oven-Roasted Green Beans

This simple side dish can pass as a healthy version of French fries and will add color to any meal. Plus you can roast the beans at the last minute while you finish setting the table.

for baby:

- Omit black pepper.
- Cut the green beans into bite-sized pieces.
- Serve 3 to 5 green beans in a small bowl or on a rimmed plate.

1	pound green beans, trimmed
2	teaspoons extra-virgin olive oil
½	teaspoon sea salt
¼	teaspoon freshly ground black pepper

1. Preheat oven to 425°. **2. Place** a jelly-roll pan in oven for 10 minutes. Place beans in a large bowl. Drizzle with oil; sprinkle with salt and pepper. Toss well to coat. Arrange green bean mixture in a single layer on preheated baking sheet. Bake at 425° for 8 minutes or until crisp-tender. **Yield:** 6 adult servings (serving size: about ⅔ cup).

CALORIES 37; FAT 1.6g (sat 0.2g, mono 1.1g, poly 0.2g); PROTEIN 1.4g; CARB 5.5g; FIBER 2.6g; CHOL 0.0mg; IRON 0.8mg; SODIUM 196mg; CALC 29mg

simple finger food steamers

This is finger food at its healthiest! Below are some ideas on good veggies to steam and serve as simple finger foods for your toddler. Steam a single vegetable or a medley of different ones for a side dish and colorful plate. You can serve these finger foods warm or chilled, so make extra to keep in the refrigerator for the next few meals.

Broccoli or cauliflower	Break into small florets, discard tough stems
Green beans	Remove strings
Sweet potato	Peel and cube
Zucchini or squash	Slice into half-moon shapes or cube
Potato	Peel and cube
Green peas	Shelled or thawed (if frozen)
Corn kernels	Thawed (if frozen)
Carrots	Peel and cube or cut into sticks

To prepare, place selected veggies in steamer basket in saucepan over boiling water. Cover and steam 7 to 10 minutes or until tender, but not soft and mushy. The smaller the cube or slice, the less time it will take to steam.

Honey-Glazed Carrots

Orange rind gives carrots a sweet, citrusy flavor, but the white pith has a bitter flavor, so be sure to avoid it when you're zesting.

for baby:
- Omit black pepper.
- Cut the carrot slices into bite-sized pieces.
- Serve spoonfuls in a small bowl or on a rimmed plate.

1½	quarts water
5	cups thinly sliced carrots
3	tablespoons chopped fresh parsley
2	tablespoons honey
½	teaspoon salt
½	teaspoon grated orange rind
¼	teaspoon freshly ground black pepper

1. Bring water to a boil in a medium saucepan. Add carrot; cook for 20 minutes or until tender. Drain well. Place carrot, parsley, and remaining ingredients in a large bowl; toss gently. **Yield:** 8 adult servings (serving size: about ½ cup).

CALORIES 51; FAT 0.2g (sat 0g, mono 0g, poly 0.1g); PROTEIN 0.8g; CARB 12.5g; FIBER 3g; CHOL 0mg; IRON 0.5mg; SODIUM 203mg; CALC 32mg

18 to 24 months

Trying New Foods

A few months ago as you spooned tiny bites of pureed peas into your little one's mouth, you may have longed for the day that baby could feed himself. Now your toddler is older, and that day has arrived. But just because he can feed himself doesn't mean that he will.

growing independence

As you probably have discovered, meals at this age are opportunities for baby to demonstrate independence by voicing preferences about what she will or won't eat. Busy little ones often don't want to take time away from playing and exploring to sit down and eat a balanced meal. Expect this to continue for the next year, and try not to let your opinionated toddler get the best of you.

Too busy to eat

Is your toddler too busy to stop and eat? Are there days when eating is the last thing that interests him? This is very common at this age, yet it's always a stressor to parents. As adults, we've been trained to eat three meals a day to stay healthy. But along the way, we forgot to listen to our body's hunger cues. Babies and toddlers, however, are much better at listening to their bodies' signals. Consequently, if they aren't hungry, they won't eat. If your child is within normal ranges on growth charts and considered healthy, child experts recommend not pressuring your toddler to eat. A healthy child will eat when she is hungry and won't starve to death from refusing food.

Food jags

One week it's bananas, the next week it's yogurt. Eating the same food meal after meal is very common at this age and will likely continue periodically for the next few years. Yet food jags always cause parents to worry that toddlers aren't getting enough nutrients in their diets. So what is a parent to do?

Actually, the less you do the better. Continue to give baby healthy meals and snacks as usual, but make sure to include baby's "food of the week." Don't make a big deal if other foods are hardly touched. If you make a big deal about baby not eating other foods, it can quickly turn into a control issue. If you don't make a big deal about it, this food will often lose its appeal after a few days.

Another trick: Try taking baby to the grocery and letting her help pick out a new fruit or vegetable. Involving toddlers in the decision-making process about meals—even if it's a small decision—can often help change the focus at mealtime to a new food.

Handling food refusals

You may also notice your toddler beginning to refuse foods that he has always eaten and loved. This is just the beginning of your baby exerting independence over food choices (and every other aspect of his life!). The key is handling each meal refusal appropriately so it doesn't grow into a control issue between you and your toddler.

tips for handling food refusals

If your child refuses a meal, try the following tips:

- Calmly remove baby's plate from the table.
- Allow baby to leave the table.
- Keep baby's plate on hand for later when he does get hungry.

inside a toddler's head

Toddlers' food preferences aren't always logical. One day they love a food; the next day they refuse to touch it. As a parent you will wear yourself out trying to read a toddler's mind. Instead of trying to figure them out, think creatively about ways to serve favorite foods that may be momentarily refused. Here are two tips from mothers that helped them circumvent potential food refusals.

- **Call it a French fry:** One mother used this tip to get her toddler to eat almost every fruit and vegetable that she could cut into a stick shape. "From green beans to apples, as long as I told Gradie it was a fry, she would devour it. I'm not sure what that says about my child's upbringing, but at least it got nutritious foods into her."

- **Give them their own container:** Another mother found that this trick helped her survive busy mornings tantrum free. "Evers knew our morning schedule was tight and sometimes used this as an opportunity to make breakfast difficult. One day he saw me pack a snack for work in a small plastic bag. He insisted on having his breakfast in one, and this continued all week. I finally purchased him small portable containers. Mornings are now about him being independent and helping put his breakfast in his container. He gets to walk around and eat breakfast, while I get things ready for work and day care. Everyone is happy—and nourished!"

- **Change the presentation:** When once-loved sliced cheese cut into bite-sized pieces was routinely refused over and over, one smart mother rolled up a cheese slice and asked her toddler if she wanted a cheese "stick." The tot eagerly reached for it, ate the cheese, and then asked for another. As this mother says, "Who knew presentation mattered so much to a toddler?"

Flavors from around the world

Cooking ethnic dishes with mild seasonings is a great way to continue to expand baby's palate. Toddlers at this age are usually still open to trying new foods—especially when they see the rest of the family eating the dish.

The recipes included in this chapter offer simple ethnic dishes with modifications to make them toddler friendly but still tasty to the rest of the family. These recipes include dishes inspired by favorite foods from Italy, Greece, Thailand, and Mexico.

Dips

Toddlers are all about being independent, which can make mealtime a challenge. But we have an answer—dips! Toddlers love the "do-it-myself" aspect of dipping and participating in an activity they've seen older kids and parents do. Give them a bowl of tasty dip, and most children this age will eat anything you put in front of them from fruit and veggies to chicken and tofu. Don't stop with ketchup though; use dips as an opportunity to get additional nutrients, protein, and fiber into baby's diet.

dip diversity

On the next few pages, we've compiled six quick and healthy dips that are sure to please baby. Parents will love them as well. In fact, many of these dips make great snacks or meal accompaniments for adults, too. Most of these dips keep for several days in the refrigerator and are great to have on hand for nutritious snacks for all ages.

Creamy Yogurt Dip

Leftover dip makes a great breakfast; top a spoonful or two of the dip with fresh fruit and a sprinkling of cereal or granola.

for your toddler:

• Serve the dip with any fruit such as grapes, strawberries, pineapple, or blueberries. Cut the fruit as needed into bite-sized pieces.

1   (7-ounce) container plain 2% low-fat Greek yogurt
1½   tablespoons honey
¼   teaspoon vanilla extract

1. Combine all ingredients in a small bowl, stirring well. Cover and chill until ready to serve. **Yield:** 3 servings (serving size: ¼ cup).

CALORIES 76; FAT 1.3g (sat 1g, mono 0g, poly 0g); PROTEIN 5.7g; CARB 11.4g; FIBER 0g; CHOL 3mg; IRON 0mg; SODIUM 22mg; CALC 60mg

Love Your Lima Beans Dip

Lima beans give this hummus-like dip a slightly sweet flavor.

for your toddler:

• Serve the dip with tender raw vegetables like pea pods and cucumber halves or slightly steamed carrot sticks and broccoli florets.

1   pound frozen baby lima beans
3   tablespoons sesame seeds, toasted
¼   cup fresh lemon juice
1   tablespoon extra-virgin olive oil
¾   teaspoon salt
1   garlic clove

1. Cook beans in boiling water 10 minutes or until very tender. Drain, reserving ½ cup cooking liquid. **2. Place** sesame seeds in a blender; process until finely ground. Add juice and remaining ingredients; process until blended. Add beans and ½ cup reserved liquid; process until almost smooth, scraping sides of blender occasionally. **Yield:** 8 servings (serving size: about ¼ cup).

CALORIES 95; FAT 3.4g (sat 0.3g, mono 1.4g, poly 0.2g); PROTEIN 4.7g; CARB 13g; FIBER 3.6g; CHOL 0mg; IRON 1.4mg; SODIUM 195mg CALC 21mg

Pumpkin Dip

Canned pumpkin makes it easy to whip up this sweet treat. Make sure to purchase 100% pure pumpkin and not pumpkin pie filling.

for your toddler:

• Serve the dip with peeled apple slices, banana slices, or cinnamon pita chips.

¾ cup (6 ounces) ⅓-less-fat cream cheese, softened
¼ cup packed brown sugar
½ cup canned pumpkin
1 tablespoon maple syrup
½ teaspoon ground cinnamon

1. Combine first 3 ingredients in a medium bowl; beat with a mixer at medium speed until well combined. Add syrup and cinnamon, and beat until smooth. Cover and chill 30 minutes before serving. **Yield:** 8 servings (serving size: ¼ cup).

CALORIES 91; FAT 4.6g (sat 3.1g, mono 0g, poly 0g); PROTEIN 2.5g; CARB 10.5g; FIBER 0.5g; CHOL 15mg; IRON 0.4mg; SODIUM 135mg; CALC 28mg

perfect world: Your toddler now has definite preferences about what foods she does and doesn't like, so you are able to plan her meals and snacks accordingly.

real world: Just when you think you know what she likes, plan on it changing. Don't be surprised if a favorite food is refused one day, yet begged for the next. The lesson for parents is to continue to offer healthy foods even if they have been refused in the past. You never know what might appeal to your toddler today!

Good-for-You Guacamole

Peas give nutrient-rich avocado a boost of fiber. For babies who like less-seasoned food, make a simple pea guacamole using only peas, avocado, and a splash of lime juice.

for your toddler:

• Serve the dip with baked whole-grain tortilla or pita, or slightly steamed carrot sticks and other veggies.
• Serve it as a spread on a tortilla; roll up the tortilla.

1   cup frozen petite green peas
1   large ripe peeled avocado, cut in half and pitted
¼   cup chopped green onions
¼   cup bottled salsa
1½   tablespoons fresh lime juice
½   teaspoon ground cumin
4   sprigs cilantro
2   garlic cloves

1. **Place** peas in a vegetable steamer. Steam, covered, 4 minutes or until peas are tender. Combine peas, avocado, and remaining ingredients in a food processor; pulse just until combined. Cover surface of guacamole with plastic wrap. Chill until ready to serve. **Yield:** 7 servings (serving size: ¼ cup).

CALORIES 51; FAT 3g (sat 0.4g, mono 1.9g, poly 0.4g); PROTEIN 1.7g; CARB 5.8g; FIBER 2.6g; CHOL 0mg; IRON 0.5mg; SODIUM 90mg; CALC 13mg

Hummus

This traditional Middle Eastern dip also makes a tasty spread on wraps and sandwiches in place of mayonnaise and mustard.

for your toddler:

• Serve the hummus with wedges of soft whole-grain pita bread or tender raw vegetables like pea pods and cucumber halves or slightly steamed carrot sticks and broccoli florets.
• Spread the hummus on a whole-wheat tortilla wrap, and roll it into "pinwheel" bites.

1   (15.5-ounce) can no-salt-added chickpeas (garbanzo beans), rinsed and drained
1   garlic clove, crushed
¼   cup water
2   tablespoons tahini (sesame seed paste)
1½   tablespoons fresh lemon juice
1   tablespoon extra-virgin olive oil
¼   teaspoon salt

1. **Place** beans and garlic in a food processor; pulse 5 times or until chopped. Add ¼ cup water and remaining ingredients; pulse until smooth, scraping down sides as needed. **Yield:** 2½ cups (serving size: ¼ cup).

CALORIES 100; FAT 5.7g (sat 0.7g, mono 2.9g, poly 1.5g); PROTEIN 3.6g; CARB 9.6g; FIBER 2.3g; CHOL 0mg; IRON 0.6mg; SODIUM 109mg; CALC 25mg

Asian Peanut Dip

Adults can use extra dip as a spread for veg-gie wraps or sandwiches made with grated carrot, sliced cucumber, and lettuce.

for your toddler:

• Serve the dip with tender raw vegetables like pea pods and cucumber halves or slightly steamed sugar snap peas, carrot sticks, and broccoli florets.

½   cup natural creamy peanut butter
⅓   cup reduced-fat, firm silken tofu
3   tablespoons brown sugar
2   tablespoons fresh lime juice
2   tablespoons low-sodium soy sauce
1   garlic clove, crushed

1. Place all ingredients in a blender; process until smooth. Store in an airtight container in refrigerator for up to 2 days. **Yield:** 8 servings (serving size: 2 tablespoons).

CALORIES 122; FAT 7.7g (sat 1.5g, mono 3.8g, poly 2.5g); PROTEIN 5.4g; CARB 7.4g; FIBER 0.5g; CHOL 0mg; IRON 0.4mg; SODIUM 131mg; CALC 19mg

nutrition note
peanut butter facts

Whether spread on a piece of whole-grain bread or an apple slice, peanut butter makes a satisfying meal or snack in a matter of minutes. Part of the reason it's so satisfying is because each tablespoon of peanut butter contains about 4 grams of protein and 8 grams of fat, most of which is heart-healthy monounsaturated and polyun-saturated fat. When buying peanut butter, be sure to choose one labeled "natural" to avoid the trans-fatty acids that come from partially hydrogenated oils, which can increase the LDL, or bad cholesterol, levels in your body. Another bonus—natural peanut butter has much less added sugar and salt.

Crispy Tofu Pad Thai

Tofu is a plant-based protein made from soybeans that takes on the flavors of the ingredients cooked with it.

for your toddler:

- Omit the Sriracha and green onions; adults can add them to their servings later, if desired.
- Serve a spoonful of noodles tossed with the sauce and 3 to 5 tofu cubes in a small bowl.
- Cut the noodles into bite-sized pieces.

1	(12.3-ounce) package reduced-fat, firm tofu, drained
1	tablespoon cornstarch
6	ounces flat uncooked rice noodles
½	cup ketchup
2	tablespoons sugar
2	tablespoons fish sauce
1	tablespoon Sriracha (hot chile sauce, such as Huy Fong)
2	tablespoons canola oil, divided
2	large eggs, lightly beaten
1	large egg white, lightly beaten
½	cup chopped green onions
2	tablespoons chopped fresh cilantro
2	tablespoons unsalted, dry-roasted peanuts, chopped
4	lime wedges

1. Cut tofu crosswise into 8 (½-inch-thick) slices. Arrange tofu on several layers of paper towels. Top with several more layers of paper towels; top with a cast-iron skillet or other heavy pan. Let stand 30 minutes. Remove tofu from paper towels. Cut tofu into ½-inch cubes, and toss with cornstarch. **2. Prepare** noodles according to package directions, omitting salt and fat. Drain well; set aside. **3. Combine** ketchup and next 3 ingredients. Heat 1 tablespoon oil in a non-stick skillet over medium-high heat. Add tofu to pan; sauté 7 minutes or until golden. Remove tofu from pan. **4. Heat** 1 teaspoon oil in pan. Add eggs and egg white; cook 30 seconds, stirring constantly. Remove from pan. Heat remaining 2 teaspoons oil in pan. Add noodles; cook 3 minutes. Stir in ketchup mixture; cook 30 seconds. Add egg mixture; cook 1 minute, stirring often. Remove from heat; stir in onions and cilantro. Top noodles with tofu; sprinkle with peanuts and serve with lime wedges. **Yield:** 4 adult servings (serving size: 1 cup noodles, ½ cup tofu, and 1½ teaspoons peanuts).

CALORIES 419; FAT 14.4g (sat 1.7g, mono 6.8g, poly 3.5g); PROTEIN 15.4g; CARB 57.5g; FIBER 2.8g; CHOL 106mg; IRON 3.3mg; SODIUM 845mg; CALC 374mg

Risotto Primavera

for your toddler:

- Cook the vegetables 2 to 3 minutes longer.
- Serve a spoonful of risotto and vegetables.
- Cut the vegetables into bite-sized pieces.

1½	teaspoons olive oil
3	cups (2 inch) diagonally cut asparagus
2	cups chopped yellow squash
¼	teaspoon salt
¼	teaspoon freshly ground black pepper
1	garlic clove, minced
1	cup water
1	(32-ounce) carton fat-free, less-sodium chicken broth 3.8 cups
1	tablespoon butter
2	cups chopped leek
1½	cups Arborio rice
½	cup (2 ounces) grated fresh Parmesan cheese, divided
1½	teaspoons fresh thyme

Risotto Primavera

1. Heat oil in a large nonstick skillet over medium-high heat. Add asparagus and next 4 ingredients; sauté 10 minutes or until vegetables are crisp-tender. Set aside; keep warm. **2. Bring** water and broth to a simmer in a medium saucepan (do not boil). Keep warm over low heat. **3. Melt** butter in a large Dutch oven over medium heat. Add leek; cook 4 minutes or until tender, stirring frequently. Add rice; cook 2 minutes, stirring constantly. Stir in 1½ cups broth mixture; cook 4 minutes or until liquid is nearly absorbed, stirring constantly. Add remaining broth mixture, ½ cup at a time, stirring constantly until each portion of broth is absorbed before adding the next (about 20 minutes total). Stir in ¼ cup cheese and thyme. **4. Top** risotto with vegetables; sprinkle with remaining ¼ cup cheese. **Yield:** 6 adult servings (serving size: ⅔ cup risotto, about ½ cup vegetables, and 2 teaspoons cheese).

CALORIES 283; FAT 6.5g (sat 2.8g, mono 1.3g, poly 0.3g); PROTEIN 11.2g; CARB 46.3g; FIBER 4.4g; CHOL 12mg; IRON 2.4mg; SODIUM 587mg; CALC 177mg

Trying New Foods **87**

Mediterranean Salmon Salad

Don't let the word "salad" in the title deter you from serving this warm mix of pasta, salmon, and vegetables to your little one.

for your toddler:

- Omit the black pepper from the fish.
- Toss a spoonful of hot orzo with a small handful of torn spinach until the spinach wilts and the mixture is cool.
- Shred a small amount of salmon and add it to the mixture. Add olives and cheese, if desired.

½	cup uncooked orzo
2	(6-ounce) salmon fillets (about 1 inch thick)
¼	teaspoon salt
¼	teaspoon dried oregano
⅛	teaspoon black pepper
Cooking spray	
2	cups torn spinach
½	cup chopped red bell pepper
¼	cup chopped green onions
4	kalamata olives, pitted and chopped
3	tablespoons fresh lemon juice
2	tablespoons crumbled feta cheese

1. Preheat broiler. **2. Cook** pasta according to package directions, omitting salt and fat. **3. Sprinkle** salmon evenly with salt, oregano, and black pepper. Place on a broiler pan coated with cooking spray. Broil 10 minutes or until fish flakes easily when tested with a fork or until desired degree of doneness. Let stand 5 minutes; break into bite-sized pieces with 2 forks. **4. Combine** pasta, salmon, spinach, and remaining ingredients in a medium bowl; toss well. **Yield:** 4 adult servings (serving size: 1 cup).

CALORIES 231; FAT 7.7g (sat 1.6g,mono 2.7g,poly 2.3g); PROTEIN 20.3g; CARB 19.3g; FIBER 1.8g; CHOL 49mg; IRON 1.3mg; SODIUM 310mg; CALC 56mg

Sweet-and-Sour Chicken

Introduce baby to the yummy taste of takeout food without all the extra fat. This homestyle sweet-and-sour chicken has a lighter, fresher tasting sauce than typical restaurant versions. Serve with steamed brown or basmati rice.

for your toddler:

- Omit the chile paste; adults can sprinkle red pepper flakes over their portions.
- Cut a piece of chicken and a spoonful of vegetables into small pieces.
- Serve it over rice in a small bowl or on a rimmed plate.

4	teaspoons cornstarch, divided
5	teaspoons low-sodium soy sauce, divided
1	teaspoon minced peeled fresh ginger
1	teaspoon dark soy sauce
2	garlic cloves, minced
1	pound skinless, boneless chicken breast, cut into 2 x ½-inch-thick pieces
½	cup fat-free, less-sodium chicken broth
1	tablespoon brown sugar
3	tablespoons ketchup
2½	tablespoons rice vinegar
2	teaspoons chile paste
1	teaspoon dark sesame oil
1	tablespoon canola oil, divided
1	cup (½-inch) diced onion
1	cup (½-inch) diced green bell pepper
1	cup (½-inch) diced red bell pepper
½	cup (1-inch) slices green onions
1	cup (½-inch) diced fresh pineapple

1. Combine 2 teaspoons cornstarch, 2 teaspoons low-sodium soy sauce, and next 3 ingredients in a medium bowl. Add chicken; stir well to coat.

Set aside. **2. Combine** broth, remaining 2 teaspoons cornstarch, remaining 1 tablespoon low-sodium soy sauce, brown sugar, and next 4 ingredients. **3. Heat** ½ teaspoon canola oil in a large skillet over medium-high heat. Add diced onion and next 3 ingredients to pan; sauté 4 minutes or until crisp-tender. Transfer to a bowl. **4. Heat** remaining 2½ teaspoons canola oil in pan. Add chicken mixture to pan, and spread in an even layer; cook, without stirring, 1 minute. Sauté an additional 3 minutes or until chicken is done. **5. Return** vegetable mixture to pan. Add soy sauce mixture and pineapple, stirring well to combine. Bring to a boil; cook 1 minute or until thickened, stirring constantly. **Yield:** 4 adult servings (serving size: about 1⅓ cup).

CALORIES 267; FAT 6.4g (sat 0.9g, mono 2.4g, poly 1.5g); PROTEIN 28.5g; CARB 25g; FIBER 3.1g; CHOL 66mg; IRON 1.9mg; SODIUM 626mg; CALC 51mg

getting out of a snacking rut

Do you feel like you're in a rut when it comes to snacks for your toddler? Try some of our suggestions:

On-the-Go Snacks:

- Small boxes of raisins
- Whole-grain cereal or natural granola bars (or those with little added sugar)
- Whole-grain pretzels or crackers
- Cheese cubes or string cheese
- Low-sugar, whole-grain dry cereal

More Filling Snacks:

- Fresh fruit or veggies with hummus or other dip
- Yogurt with low-fat granola
- Half of a cheese, turkey, or peanut butter sandwich
- Whole-grain mini bagel with peanut butter
- Applesauce and graham crackers

Frittata with Broccoli, Potato, and Leeks

for your toddler:

- Cut a small wedge into bite-sized pieces.
- Serve it on a rimmed plate.

1   teaspoon butter
2   cups thinly sliced leek (about 2 large)
1   (10-ounce) package frozen chopped broccoli, thawed
⅓   cup fat-free milk
2   tablespoons finely chopped fresh basil
½   teaspoon salt
¼   teaspoon black pepper
4   large eggs
4   large egg whites
1   cup chopped cooked peeled red potato
⅔   cup (2.7 ounces) shredded fontina cheese, divided
Cooking spray
1½   tablespoons dry breadcrumbs

1. Preheat oven to 350°. **2. Melt** butter in a large nonstick skillet over medium heat. Add leek; sauté 6 minutes. **3. Press** broccoli between several layers of paper towels to remove excess moisture. Combine milk and next 5 ingredients, stirring with a whisk. Add leek mixture, broccoli, potato, and ⅓ cup cheese. Pour into a 9½-inch-deep dish pie plate coated with cooking spray. Sprinkle with remaining ⅓ cup cheese and breadcrumbs. Bake at 350° for 25 minutes or until center is set. **4. Preheat** broiler. **5. Place** frittata on center rack of oven; broil 4 minutes or until golden brown. Remove from oven; let stand 5 minutes. Cut into wedges. **Yield:** 6 servings (serving size: 1 wedge).

CALORIES 185; FAT 7.7g (sat 3.7g, mono 2.6g, poly 0.9g); PROTEIN 13.2g; CARB 15.8g; FIBER 2.7g; CHOL 137mg; IRON 2mg; SODIUM 423mg; CALC 153mg

Herbed Chicken Parmesan

We recommend orzo, but you can serve it with spaghetti or angel hair pasta instead.

for your toddler:

- Cut a chicken tender into bite-sized pieces.
- Serve the chicken and a spoonful of pasta in a bowl.
- Sprinkle the pasta with cheese.

½   cup (2 ounces) grated fresh Parmesan cheese, divided
½   cup dry breadcrumbs
2   tablespoons minced fresh parsley
1   teaspoon dried basil
2   large egg whites, lightly beaten
1   pound chicken breast tenders
1   tablespoon olive oil
1½   cups jarred tomato-basil pasta sauce
2   teaspoons balsamic vinegar
3   (0.6-ounce) slices provolone cheese, cut into thin strips

1. Preheat broiler. **2. Combine** ¼ cup Parmesan cheese, breadcrumbs, parsley, and basil in a shallow dish; place egg whites in a bowl. Dip each chicken tender in egg whites; dredge in breadcrumb mixture. **3. Heat** oil in a large nonstick skillet over medium-high heat. Add chicken; cook 5 minutes on each side or until chicken is done. Remove pan from heat. **4. Combine** pasta sauce and vinegar in a microwave-safe bowl. Cover with plastic wrap; vent. Microwave at HIGH 2 minutes or until thoroughly heated. Pour sauce over chicken in pan. Sprinkle remaining ¼ cup Parmesan and layer provolone over chicken. Cover, and cook 2 minutes or until cheeses melt. **Yield:** 4 adult servings (serving size: about 2 chicken tenders and about ⅓ cup sauce).

CALORIES 365; FAT 13.8g (sat 5.3g, mono 3.8g, poly 0.8g); PROTEIN 41g; CARB 17.9g; FIBER 2.2g; CHOL 85mg; IRON 1.7mg; SODIUM 861mg; CALC 383mg

at our house

Persistence pays

When my son, Elliott, was about 6 months old, we started introducing him to baby food. He had been showing a lot of interest in our "people food" for weeks, and I was so excited about him reaching this milestone. Drum roll, please: We gave him a bite of jarred peaches (mixed with a little baby cereal). He made a terrible face and promptly spit it out. I was crestfallen! I just knew that I was going to have one of those I-want-chicken fingers-and-fries-only toddlers.

But I was determined not to give Elliott over to McDonald's without a fight. So we served him peaches again. And again. And again. Pretty soon, he was a  peach-eating machine. Same story with most of the other fruits and vegetables we gave him in the next year, including some that don't really appeal to me much. Now Elliott will eat pretty much anything we serve him. We definitely learned firsthand that persistence is the key.

—Marilyn Smith, mom of Elliott, 20 months

Chicken Souvlaki with Tzatziki Sauce

Tzatziki is a traditional Greek yogurt–based sauce flavored with lemon, garlic, and crisp cucumber. Let toddlers dip halved cucumber slices, chunks of tomato, or whole-wheat pita bread into extra tzatziki. Serve this dish with whole-wheat or flavored couscous.

for your toddler:

- Remove 1 to 2 chicken and zucchini pieces from the skewers.
- Cut the chicken and zucchini into bite-sized pieces.
- Serve the chicken and zucchini with a small spoonful of tzatziki sauce for dipping on a rimmed plate.

6   tablespoons fresh lemon juice
3   teaspoons chopped fresh oregano or 1 teaspoon dried oregano
4   teaspoons olive oil
4   garlic cloves, minced
1   teaspoon salt
1   pound skinless, boneless chicken breast halves, cut into bite-sized pieces
½   cup peeled, shredded, seeded cucumber
½   cup plain low-fat yogurt
1   tablespoon fresh lemon juice
1   garlic clove, minced
¼   teaspoon salt
2   zucchini, quartered lengthwise and cut into ½-inch-thick slices
Cooking spray

1. To prepare souvlaki, combine first 5 ingredients in a large zip-top plastic bag. Add chicken to bag; seal. Marinate in refrigerator for 30 minutes, turning bag once. **2. Prepare** grill to medium-high heat. **3. While** chicken marinates, combine cucumber and next 4 ingredients, stirring well. **4. To prepare** skewers, remove chicken from bag; discard marinade. Thread chicken and zucchini alternately onto each of 4 (8-inch) skewers. **5. Place** skewers on a grill rack coated with cooking spray; grill 10 minutes or until chicken is done, turning once. **6. Serve** tzatziki sauce with chicken skewers. **Yield:** 4 adult servings (serving size: 2 skewers and about ¼ cup tzatziki sauce).

CALORIES 213; FAT 6.6g (sat 1.3g, mono 3.8g, poly 0.9g); PROTEIN 29.3g; CARB 9.3g; FIBER 1.4g; CHOL 67mg; IRON 1.3mg; SODIUM 831mg; CALC 95mg

Chipotle Pork Soft Tacos with Pineapple Salsa

Pork, a common taco filling throughout Latin America, takes well to spices. When serving these soft tacos to younger children, spoon the pork and salsa into a tortilla, roll the tortilla tightly, and then cut it into small bite-sized pieces.

for your toddler:

- When making the salsa, cut extra fruit into small bite-sized pieces for baby.
- Omit the black pepper and chipotle peppers; after removing the baby's pork, parents can add peppers at end of simmering in Step 2.
- Cut the pork into bite-sized pieces.
- Serve the pork and fruit pieces as finger foods on a plate with a warmed corn tortilla.

2	cups minced pineapple
1	cup minced apple
¼	cup minced shallots
2	tablespoons chopped cilantro
1	tablespoon fresh lime juice
½	teaspoon ground cumin
¼	teaspoon salt
1	tablespoon canola oil
1	cup thinly sliced yellow onion
2	garlic cloves, minced
1½	pounds pork tenderloin, cut lengthwise and thinly sliced crosswise
½	cup fat-free, less-sodium chicken broth
1	tablespoon cider vinegar
1	teaspoon dried oregano
1	teaspoon ground cumin
½	teaspoon salt
½	teaspoon freshly ground black pepper
12	cherry tomatoes, quartered
2	chipotle chiles, canned in adobo sauce, chopped (about 2 tablespoons)
12	(6-inch) corn tortillas

1. To prepare salsa, combine first 7 ingredients in a medium bowl; stir until well blended. Cover and chill. **2. To prepare** tacos, heat oil in a large nonstick skillet over medium heat. Add onion to pan; cook 2 minutes or until tender. Add garlic; cook 30 seconds. Add pork to pan; cook 4 minutes or until pork is no longer pink, stirring occasionally. Stir in broth and next 7 ingredients. Cover, reduce heat, and simmer 10 minutes. Uncover; simmer 10 minutes or until liquid is nearly evaporated. **3. Warm** tortillas according to package directions. Serve pork mixture with tortillas and salsa. **Yield:** 6 adult servings (serving size: 2 tortillas, ⅔ cup pork mixture, and ½ cup salsa).

CALORIES 391; FAT 8.3g (sat 1.8g, mono 3.6g, poly 2g); PROTEIN 29.3g; CARB 50.8g; FIBER 6.9g; CHOL 74mg; IRON 3.6mg; SODIUM 420mg; CALC 161mg

Moroccan-Style Braised Beef with Carrots and Couscous

Tender beef and a blend of North African spices render a hearty stew that's full of flavor—and nutrients—for the entire family. If you don't have an immersion blender for Step 2, you can remove some of the mixture and puree it in a blender or food processor—or skip this step and have a slightly less-thick stew.

for your toddler:

• Serve a spoonful of the couscous and the stew mixture in a small bowl.

• Cut the vegetables and beef into bite-sized pieces, and then stir them together to make spooning easier for baby.

another option for your toddler:

• Remove a few beef chunks and carrots, cut them into small pieces, and serve them as finger foods.

• Serve the beef and carrots with a bowl of couscous.

2	teaspoons olive oil
1	pound lean beef stew meat, cut into 1-inch cubes
¼	teaspoon salt
3	cups thinly sliced onion
4	garlic cloves, chopped
2	teaspoons ground cumin
2	teaspoons ground turmeric
2	teaspoons paprika
1	teaspoon ground ginger
2	(14-ounce) cans less-sodium beef broth
¼	cup packed dried apricots
⅛	teaspoon salt
⅛	teaspoon black pepper
2	cups diagonally sliced peeled carrot (about 4 carrots)
2	tablespoons water (optional)
¼	cup chopped fresh flat-leaf parsley
2	teaspoons olive oil
1	garlic clove, crushed
½	teaspoon salt
¼	teaspoon ground turmeric

couscous

⅓	cup less-sodium beef broth
⅓	cup water
⅔	cup uncooked couscous
¼	cup chopped green onions

1. To prepare beef, heat 2 teaspoons oil in a large saucepan over medium-high heat. Sprinkle beef with ¼ teaspoon salt. Add beef to pan, and cook 4 minutes or until beef is browned on all sides, turning occasionally. Transfer beef to a bowl; cover and keep warm. **2. Add** 3 cups onion to pan; cook 10 minutes or until tender, stirring frequently. Add 4 chopped garlic cloves and next 4 ingredients; cook 1 minute, stirring constantly. Add 2 cans broth; bring to a boil. Add apricots; reduce heat, and simmer 5 minutes. Cover and cook over medium-low heat 30 minutes. Using an immersion blender in pan, puree onion mixture. Stir in ⅛ teaspoon salt and ⅛ teaspoon pepper. **3. Return** beef to onion mixture; cook over medium-low heat 1 hour or until beef is tender. Add carrot to pan; cover and cook 15 minutes or until carrot is tender, adding 2 tablespoons water, if desired, to thin sauce. Stir in parsley. **4. While** beef cooks, heat 2 teaspoons oil in a small saucepan over medium heat. Add crushed garlic clove, ½ teaspoon salt, and ¼ teaspoon turmeric. Stir in ⅓ cup broth and ⅓ cup water; bring to a boil. Gradually stir in couscous. Remove from heat. Cover and let stand 5 minutes; fluff with a fork. Stir in green onions. Spoon couscous onto 4 plates. Top evenly with beef stew. **Yield:** 4 adult servings (serving size: 1 cup stew and ½ cup couscous).

CALORIES 439; FAT 14.6g (sat 4.1g, mono 7.4g, poly 1.3g); PROTEIN 32g; CARB 43.7g; FIBER 6g; CHOL 71mg; IRON 5.7mg; SODIUM 681mg; CALC 91mg

ethnic flavors

Cooking ethnic dishes, such as this Moroccan-inspired dish, is a great way to introduce your toddler to new flavors and expand her palate.

Pork and Squash Stir-Fry

Pork and Squash Stir-Fry

*Butternut squash is a unique addition to stir-fry that pairs well with Asian seasonings.
Serve it over cooked rice or noodles.*

for your toddler:

- Reserve 3 or 4 cubes of squash following Step 1.
- Sauté 1 strip of pork in a separate pan until done.
- Cut the squash into bite-sized pieces, and shred the pork.
- Serve the pork and squash with rice.

5   cups (½-inch) cubed peeled butternut squash
    (about 2 pounds)
2   tablespoons peanut oil
2   tablespoons coarsely grated orange rind

1   tablespoon minced peeled fresh ginger
1   (3-inch) cinnamon stick, broken
1¼   pounds pork tenderloin, trimmed and cut into
     2-inch strips
2   tablespoons sugar
3   tablespoons low-sodium soy sauce
2   tablespoons balsamic vinegar
2   tablespoons red wine vinegar
1   teaspoon cornstarch
¼   teaspoon salt
1   cup chopped green onions

Even if you've made every bite of food your child has ever eaten and avoided sugary cookies at all costs, it's highly unlikely your toddler will make it much longer without discovering sweets. Children quickly catch on that these foods taste really good but that parents don't want their kids to have them too often. The truth is that sweets or foods with added sugar are fine in small amounts, but it's essential for parents to teach and model the concept of moderation and portion control for their children. A small dessert every now and then is fine—a cookie after every meal is not.

1. **Place** squash in a large microwave-safe bowl. Add water to a depth of 1 inch. Cover with plastic wrap; vent. Microwave at HIGH 8 minutes or until tender. Drain and set aside. 2. **Heat** oil in a large nonstick skillet over medium heat. Add orange rind, ginger, and cinnamon stick pieces; cook 1 minute, stirring constantly. Remove and discard cinnamon stick pieces. 3. **Increase** heat to medium-high. Add pork to pan, and sauté 4 minutes or until browned. Combine sugar and next 5 ingredients, stirring with a whisk. Add sugar mixture to pan; cook 2 minutes or until sauce is slightly thickened, stirring constantly. Add squash; tossing to coat. Stir in green onions. **Yield:** 6 adult servings (serving size: 1 cup).

CALORIES 257; FAT 7.9g (sat 1.9g, mono 3.6g, poly 1.9g); PROTEIN 21.9g; CARB 25.9g; FIBER: 6.2g; CHOL 61mg; IRON 2.5mg; SODIUM 423mg; CALC 84mg

Hoisin Pork Tenderloin

Cooked pork tenderloin is tender and easy for baby to chew when it's cut into small pieces or shredded. Bottled hoisin sauce can be found in the Asian section of your grocery store. Serve this flavorful version with rice or pasta and steamed sugar snap peas.

for your toddler:

- Cut the pork into small bite-sized pieces or shred it.
- Serve it on a rimmed plate with other prepared side dishes.

¼ cup hoisin sauce
2 tablespoons sliced green onions
2 tablespoons low-sodium soy sauce
1 tablespoon rice wine vinegar
2 garlic cloves, minced
1 (1-pound) pork tenderloin, trimmed
Cooking spray
1 tablespoon sesame seeds

1. **Combine** first 5 ingredients in a large zip-top plastic bag; add pork to bag. Seal and marinate in refrigerator 2 hours, turning bag once. 2. **Preheat** oven to 425°. 3. **Remove** pork from bag, reserving marinade. Place pork on the rack of a broiler pan or roasting pan coated with cooking spray; place rack in pan. Bake at 425° for 15 minutes. Sprinkle pork with sesame seeds; bake an additional 5 minutes or until a thermometer registers 160° (slightly pink). Place pork on a cutting board; let stand 10 minutes. Cut into ½-inch-thick slices. 4. **Pour** reserved marinade into a small saucepan; bring to a boil. Cook until reduced to ⅓ cup (about 2 minutes); serve with pork. **Yield:** 4 adult servings (serving size: 3 ounces pork and about 4 teaspoons sauce).

CALORIES 194; FAT 5.8g (sat 1.7g, mono 2.2g, poly 1.1g); PROTEIN 25.4g; CARB 8.7g; FIBER 0.9g; CHOL 68mg; IRON 2mg; SODIUM 574mg; CALC 37mg

Zucchini with Corn and Cilantro

for your toddler:

- Omit the black pepper; parents can it add at the table, if desired.
- Serve a spoonful as a side with any meat, fish, poultry, or tofu.

1	teaspoon olive oil
1	pound zucchini, cut into ¾-inch cubes
1	cup frozen whole-kernel corn
1	tablespoon chopped fresh cilantro
1	teaspoon fresh lime juice
¼	teaspoon salt
⅛	teaspoon freshly ground black pepper

1. Heat oil in a large nonstick skillet over medium-high heat. Add zucchini and corn; cook, stirring occasionally, 7 minutes or until zucchini is crisp-tender. **2. Remove** from heat; stir in cilantro and remaining ingredients. **Yield:** 4 adult servings (serving size: ¾ cup).

CALORIES 62; FAT 1.6g (sat 0.2g, mono 0.9g, poly 0.3g); PROTEIN 2.6g; CARB 12g; FIBER 2.4g; CHOL 0mg; IRON 0.7mg; SODIUM 152mg; CALC 19mg

Pomegranate Gelatin with Fruit

Replace the popular sugary store-bought gelatin dessert with this nutritious jiggly dessert or snack.

for your toddler:

- Serve a spoonful in a small bowl.
- Cut the gelatin into bite-sized pieces.

2	envelopes unflavored gelatin
2	cups pomegranate juice, divided
3	tablespoons honey
1	cup coarsely chopped strawberries

1. Sprinkle gelatin over ½ cup pomegranate juice in a medium bowl. Let stand 1 minute. **2. While** gelatin mixture stands, combine remaining 1½ cups pomegranate juice and honey into a small saucepan. Bring to a boil. Add boiling juice mixture to gelatin mixture, stirring with a whisk until gelatin dissolves. Pour gelatin mixture into an 8-inch square dish; refrigerate 20 minutes or until the consistency of unbeaten egg white. Stir in strawberries. Refrigerate 40 minutes or until firm. **Yield:** 8 adult servings (serving size: ⅓ cup).

CALORIES 67; FAT 0.1g (sat 0g, mono 0g, poly 0g); PROTEIN 0.4g; CARB 17.1g; FIBER 0.4g; CHOL 0mg; IRON 0.2mg; SODIUM 9mg; CALC 14mg

Three-Grain Pilaf

Quinoa, a grain that looks like round sesame seeds, contains more protein than other grains. When paired with rice and millet, it provides a great nutty flavor.

for your toddler:

- Serve a spoonful as a side dish with meat, fish, poultry, or tofu.

2	tablespoons butter
½	cup finely chopped green onions
1	cup uncooked basmati rice
½	cup uncooked quinoa
½	cup uncooked millet
3	cups vegetable broth
¼	teaspoon salt

1. Melt butter in a large nonstick skillet over medium heat. Add onions; cook 2 minutes. Add rice, quinoa, and millet; cook 3 minutes, stirring frequently. Stir in broth and salt. Bring to a boil; cover, reduce heat, and simmer 20 minutes or until liquid is absorbed. **Yield:** 6 adult servings (serving size: 1 cup).

CALORIES 275; FAT 6.1g (sat 2.5g, mono 1.2g, poly 0.3g); PROTEIN 7.8g; CARB 50.9g; FIBER 2.4g; CHOL 10mg; IRON 2.4mg; SODIUM 636mg; CALC 16mg

Sweet Potato Steak Fries

Baked up crispy and golden, this nutritious side is a treat for all ages.

for your toddler:

• Cut the fries into bite-sized pieces, or let baby pick them up whole.

2   pounds sweet potatoes, cut into ¼-inch-thick x ¾-inch-wide strips

1   tablespoon olive oil

1   teaspoon dried oregano

¾   teaspoon salt

Cooking spray

1. Preheat oven to 450°. **2. Combine** first 4 ingredients in a large bowl; toss well. Arrange potatoes in a single layer on a large baking sheet coated with cooking spray. Bake at 450° for 18 minutes or until lightly browned. **Yield:** 6 adult servings (serving size: ⅔ cup).

CALORIES 170; FAT 2.6g (sat 0.4g, mono 1.8g, poly 0.3g); PROTEIN 2.7g; CARB 34.4g; FIBER 5.2g; CHOL 0mg; IRON 1.2mg; SODIUM 421mg; CALC 56mg

2 to 3 years

Healthy Food Habits

In what may feel like the blink of an eye,
your baby has turned into a small person
with a personality, a curious mind, and
lots of opinions.

learning healthy habits

Though you've witnessed behavior on more than one occasion that exemplifies why this age is called the "terrible twos," when your toddler isn't exerting her independence, she wants nothing more than to please you. This eagerness to please makes this stage a very impressionable period and a great time to continue modeling healthy behaviors as well as to begin teaching healthy habits.

A healthy way of life

Toddlers are constantly watching what their parents and siblings do, and they have already begun to pattern behaviors after what they see. The best way to teach good nutrition and health is to model healthy behaviors. If you expect your child to eat fruits and vegetables, then you should be filling your plate with them, too. The same is true for physical activity. Set aside time each day to be active with your toddler—run around and play games in the backyard or park, walk together as a family after dinner, or play with the dog. Toddlers need the same things as adults to stay healthy—a balanced diet and an active lifestyle.

Nutrition recommendations for toddlers

MyPyramid eating plans are available for ages 2 and up. You can find these guidelines, which are issued by the United States Department of Agriculture (USDA) in accordance with the Dietary Guidelines for Americans, on the MyPyramid Web site (www.mypyramid.gov), and you can customize them to your child's age and activity level (and your needs, too). The Web site is a great resource for parents seeking specific food-group recommendations and serving sizes.

Based on MyPyramid recommendations, a toddler between the age of 2 and 3 needs approximately the following each day:

- 3 ounces of grains, at least half of which should be whole grains (1 ounce is equal to 1 slice of bread or ½ cup of rice or cereal)
- 1 cup vegetables
- 1 cup fruit (no more than ¾ cup fruit juice)
- 2 cups milk (1% or skim)
- 2 ounces meat and beans
- 3 teaspoons oil

Avoid giving your child foods with added less-healthy fats, such as butter, fried foods, sausage, bacon, and desserts. Instead, aim for your child to get a moderate amount of fat from vegetable oils and foods like avocados and nuts. Also limit foods with added sugars like soft drinks, fruit drinks and punches, ice cream, and candy. Being physically active is important, too. That's why MyPyramid recommends limiting television time and encouraging your little one to run and jump in active play several times a day.

Channel your toddler's independence

Though your toddler has matured a lot over the past six months, you should still expect him to express opinions about what he eats every now and then. This often occurs not because he has developed strong food preferences, but because he has learned that he has some control over what he eats when he exerts his opinion. If you're not careful, this can quickly become a daily power struggle between you and your independent little one. Here are two easy solutions to prevent (or at least offset) power struggles during the 2- to 3-year age range.

• **Offer options.** One of the easiest ways to avoid power struggles with your toddler about eating is to give your child choices. Offer your child healthy options for meals and snacks, and then let her choose which one to eat. For example, give her the choice of oatmeal or a muffin at breakfast. Be sure to limit the choices to just two or three options—any more than that can overwhelm toddlers.

• **Get crazy.** Another trick is to take the emphasis off the food at mealtime by adding a different or unusual element to your normal routine. This can mean changing your meal location or food options. For example, if you sense a standoff brewing before lunch, tell your toddler that you're going to have a picnic in the backyard or even on a blanket on the living room floor. Or try serving breakfast for dinner. Routine-loving toddlers will think mommy's "crazy" idea is lots of fun—and you will have avoided a power struggle.

Letting little hands help

Letting your toddler help prepare food in the kitchen is a great way to involve your child in the meal as well as initiate a lifelong interest in cooking and nutrition. Though there are limited things that they can do at this age, toddlers love being able to help with even the most minute tasks. Another plus: toddlers who help prepare a dish are much more likely to eat it later on. In this chapter, we have identified a few ways your toddler can help with most of the recipes. Here are a few general kitchen tasks for younger children:

• Help gather ingredients from a low shelf in the pantry
• Add measured ingredients to a mixing bowl
• Stir ingredients
• Sprinkle raisins or nuts into a batter

Breakfast Fig and Nut "Cookies"

These oversized cookies are more like muffin tops, but calling them cookies makes them seem more fun. These healthy treats make a great breakfast or snack when they're paired with a glass of milk. Unprocessed bran is usually found near the hot cereals in the grocery; if you can't find it, substitute oat bran or crushed bran-flake cereal.

let your toddler help by:

- Pouring the measured figs and cranberries into a bowl.
- Stirring the ingredients in Step 3.
- Pouring the measured almonds into the batter.

¾	cup packed brown sugar
¼	cup butter, melted
2	large eggs
¼	cup finely chopped dried figs
¼	cup sweetened dried cranberries
1	teaspoon vanilla extract
4.5	ounces all-purpose flour (about 1 cup)
2.4	ounces whole-wheat flour (about ½ cup)
½	cup unprocessed bran
½	teaspoon baking soda
¼	teaspoon ground cinnamon
¼	teaspoon ground allspice
¼	cup sliced almonds
2	teaspoons granulated sugar

1. Preheat oven to 350°. **2. Combine** first 3 ingredients in a large bowl. Stir in figs, cranberries, and vanilla. **3. Weigh** or lightly spoon flours into dry measuring cups; level with a knife. Combine flours, bran, and next 3 ingredients in a bowl, stirring with a whisk. Add flour mixture to egg mixture, stirring just until moist. Gently fold in almonds. **4. Drop** by level ¼-cup measures 4 inches apart on 2 baking sheets lined with parchment paper. Sprinkle evenly with granulated sugar. Bake at 350° for 12 minutes or until almost set. Cool 2 minutes on pans. Remove from pans; cool completely on wire racks. **Yield:** 10 servings (serving size: 1 "cookie").

CALORIES 211; FAT 7.1g (sat 3.3g, mono 2.4g, poly 0.8g); PROTEIN 4.5g; CARB 33.2g; FIBER 3.4g; CHOL 54mg; IRON 1.8mg; SODIUM 115mg; CALC 37mg

Breakfast Fig and Nut "Cookies"

nutrition note
the scoop on sugar

Sugar often gets a bad rap—but not all sugars are bad. In fact, some are essential to a healthy diet. The key is understanding the different types and where they are found.

• **Natural sugars:** These sugars are found naturally in fruits and dairy products; they provide your body with energy, vitamins, minerals, and fiber. Don't worry about these sugars since they're found in healthy, nutritious foods.

• **Added sugars:** These are sugars that have been added during manufacturing or processing. They may be from a natural source, like honey or raw sugar, or a highly processed source, like high fructose corn syrup. Added sugars are often found in sodas, cookies, candy, ice cream, fruit punches, and fruit drinks and contribute to obesity, type 2 diabetes, and heart disease. Adults should eat no more than 8 teaspoons of added sugar per day—the amount found in a small can of soda. Children need even less, and foods with added sugar should be discouraged since they offer little nutritional benefit and may be eaten in place of healthier options.

The confusing part to the sugar story is that food labels only list "sugars" and do not differentiate between natural and added sugars. To determine if a food has added sugar, check the ingredient list for the following sweeteners: brown sugar, corn sweetener, corn syrup, dextrose, fructose, fruit juice concentrates, glucose, high fructose corn syrup, honey, invert sugar, lactose, maltose, malt syrup, molasses, raw sugar, sucrose, and sugar syrup.

Maple-Almond Granola

It's impossible to predict what your 2-year-old will want for breakfast each morning, which is why granola can be a great option. Serve it with yogurt or milk for breakfast, or take it along for a tasty snack on the go.

let your toddler help by:

• Looking for and gathering the ingredients.
• Pouring the measured oats and almonds into a mixing bowl.
• Spooning the cooled granola into a storage container.

4	cups regular oats
¼	cup slivered almonds
1½	teaspoons ground cinnamon
¼	teaspoon salt
⅓	cup water
⅓	cup honey
⅓	cup maple syrup
2	tablespoons brown sugar
2	tablespoons canola oil
Cooking spray	
1	cup minced dried apricots
1	cup raisins

1. Preheat oven to 325°. **2. Combine** first 4 ingredients in a large bowl. **3. Combine** water and next 4 ingredients in a small saucepan; bring to a boil. Pour over oat mixture; toss to coat. Spread oat mixture on a jelly-roll pan coated with cooking spray. Bake at 325° for 35 minutes or until golden, stirring every 10 minutes. Place in a large bowl; stir in apricots and raisins. Cool completely. **Yield:** 24 servings (serving size: ¼ cup). **Note:** Store in an airtight container for up to a week.

CALORIES 129; FAT 2.8g (sat 0.3g, mono 1.4g, poly 0.7g); PROTEIN 2.7g; CARB 25.7g; FIBER 1.9g; CHOL 0mg; IRON 1.2mg; SODIUM 28mg; CALC 20mg

Alphabet Chicken Soup

Your toddler will love finding and recognizing letters in their soup. Look for whole-wheat alphabet pasta for added fiber and vitamins.

let your toddler help by:

• Identifying and gathering the vegetables.

1	tablespoon vegetable oil
1	medium onion, chopped
2	carrots, chopped
2	celery ribs, chopped
2	garlic cloves, minced
2	(32-ounce) containers fat-free, less-sodium chicken broth
2	cups chopped cooked chicken
¼	teaspoon dried thyme
½	cup uncooked alphabet-shaped pasta

1. Heat oil in a Dutch oven over medium-high heat until hot. Add onion, carrot, and celery to pan. Sauté vegetables 5 minutes; add garlic, and sauté 1 minute or until vegetables are tender and mixture smells good. Stir in broth, chicken, and thyme. Bring to a boil; reduce heat, and simmer, stirring occasionally, 15 minutes. Stir in pasta, and cook 8 minutes or just until pasta is tender. **Yield:** 10 adult servings (serving size: 1 cup).

CALORIES 111; FAT 3.5g (sat 0.7g, mono 1.3g, poly 1.1g); PROTEIN 12g; CARB 7.9g; FIBER 0.8g; CHOL 25mg; IRON 0.6mg; SODIUM 562mg; CALC 16mg

Butternut-Beef Chili

This chili recipe is the perfect way to serve your toddler some extra veggies in a comfort food classic. Adults can top their bowls with chopped green onions and cilantro.

let your toddler help by:

• Identifying and gathering the vegetables.
• Helping rinse the beans in a colander.

1	small butternut squash (2 pounds)
1	pound ground round
1	cup chopped onion
1	cup chopped green bell pepper
½	cup water
3	cups chopped tomato (about 2 large)
2	tablespoons tomato paste
1½	teaspoons dried oregano
1½	teaspoons ground cumin
1½	teaspoons chili powder
½	teaspoon salt
2	garlic cloves, minced
1	(14-ounce) can fat-free, less-sodium beef broth
1	(16-ounce) can kidney beans, rinsed and drained

1. Pierce squash several times with a small knife. Microwave at HIGH for 2½ minutes; cool slightly. Peel squash. Cut squash in half, scoop out seeds and pulp. Cut squash into ½-inch pieces to measure 3 cups. **2. Combine** ground round, onion, and bell pepper in a Dutch oven, and cook over medium-high heat for 5 minutes or until beef is browned, stirring to crumble. Drain. **3. Return** meat mixture to pan. Stir in squash, ½ cup water, and remaining ingredients. Bring to a boil; reduce heat, and simmer 20 minutes or until squash is tender, stirring occasionally. Ladle soup into bowls. **Yield:** 6 adult servings (serving size: 1⅔ cups soup).

CALORIES 234; FAT 3.7g (sat 1.5g, mono 1.4g, poly 0.4g); PROTEIN 22.2g; CARB 30.8g; FIBER 8g; CHOL 41mg; IRON 4mg; SODIUM 608mg; CALC 103mg

kids in the kitchen

Some recipes, such as Alphabet Chicken Soup and Butternut-Beef Chili, have few tasks toddlers can help with safely. Don't let that stop you from involving your child in meal preparation and cooking. Remember that they don't necessarily have to have their hands in the food to feel like they are helping out. Toddlers just want to feel a part of what you're doing, so talk with your child about what you're doing while you complete adult-only kitchen tasks. Toddlers also love watching from afar (or far away from hot stoves and pots) while they stand on low step stools or stools with sides especially designed for toddlers to participate safely in the kitchen.

Alphabet Chicken Soup

kitchen tip

Quesadillas are fun finger food and a great way to get your toddler to eat veggies. Offer him a small spoonful of the salsa—he might surprise you and like it!

Black Bean Quesadillas with Warm Corn Salsa

Black Bean Quesadillas with Warm Corn Salsa

let your toddler help by:

- Helping rinse the beans in a colander.
- Placing the tortillas on the baking sheet.
- Sprinkling the cheese on the tortillas and bean mixture.

1 tablespoon olive oil
2 cups chopped plum tomatoes (about 6 medium)
1 (15-ounce) can black beans, rinsed and drained
2 cups bagged baby spinach leaves
4 (8-inch) whole-wheat flour tortillas
Cooking spray
1 cup (4 ounces) preshredded reduced-fat Mexican blend cheese
1 cup frozen whole-kernel corn
1 cup chopped red bell pepper
¼ cup chopped fresh cilantro
2 tablespoons fresh lime juice

1. Preheat broiler. **2. Heat** oil in a large nonstick skillet over medium-high heat. Add tomato and beans; sauté 3 minutes. Add spinach; sauté 3 minutes or until liquid evaporates, stirring occasionally. Remove from heat; mash beans slightly. **3. Place** tortillas on a baking sheet coated with cooking spray. Top each tortilla with ½ cup bean mixture and ¼ cup cheese; fold in half. Lightly coat tops with cooking spray. Broil 3 minutes or until cheese melts and tortillas begin to brown. Cut each tortilla into 3 wedges. **4. While** quesadillas broil, combine corn and remaining ingredients in a small saucepan. Cook over medium heat for 2 minutes or until warm, stirring frequently. Serve warm salsa with quesadillas. **Yield:** 4 servings (serving size: 3 quesadilla wedges and about ½ cup salsa).

CALORIES 271; FAT 12.5g (sat 3.6g, mono 2.6g, poly 0.6g); PROTEIN 17.4g; CARB 30.6g; FIBER 9.3g; CHOL 10mg; IRON 2.7mg; SODIUM 649mg; CALC 311mg

Peanut Butter–Banana Spirals

In this recipe, peanut butter stars with banana and yogurt, and we added wheat germ for crunch and a nutritional boost. If you can't find honey-crunch wheat germ, plain wheat germ will work fine. Pack these for lunch or a snack.

let your toddler help by:

- Arranging the banana slices on top of the peanut butter mixture.
- Sprinkling the wheat germ over the banana slices.

3 tablespoons vanilla low-fat yogurt
2 tablespoons natural peanut butter
1½ teaspoons orange juice
1 small banana, sliced
1 (8-inch) whole-wheat flour tortilla
1½ teaspoons honey-crunch wheat germ
Dash of ground cinnamon

1. Combine yogurt and peanut butter, stirring until smooth. Drizzle orange juice over banana slices, tossing gently to coat. **2. Spread** peanut butter mixture over tortilla, leaving a ½-inch border. Arrange banana slices, in a single layer, over peanut butter mixture. Sprinkle wheat germ and cinnamon over banana slices. Roll up tortilla; cut into 3 pieces. **Yield:** 3 serving (serving size: 1 piece).

CALORIES 129; FAT 7g (sat 0.9g, mono 2.7g, poly 1.8g); PROTEIN 5.3g; CARB 14g; FIBER 2.6g; CHOL 1mg; IRON 0.7mg; SODIUM 124mg; CALC 55mg

Oatmeal-Crusted Chicken Tenders

Using oatmeal in the breading adds crunch to these chicken tenders, which are sure to be a hit with adults and children alike. Serve with commercial honey mustard or light ranch dressing for dipping.

let your toddler help by:

• Identifying and gathering the ingredients.

1	cup old-fashioned oats
¾	cup (3 ounces) grated fresh Parmesan cheese
1	teaspoon chopped fresh thyme
½	teaspoon salt
¼	teaspoon freshly ground black pepper
1	pound chicken breast tenders

Cooking spray

1. Preheat oven to 450°. **2. Place** oats in a food processor, and process 20 seconds or until coarsely ground. Add cheese and next 3 ingredients. Pulse to combine, and place in a shallow bowl. **3. Place** each chicken breast tender between 2 sheets of heavy-duty plastic wrap; pound to ¼-inch thickness using a meat mallet or small heavy skillet. Coat both sides of tenders with cooking spray; dredge tenders in oat mixture. Place tenders on a baking sheet coated with cooking spray. Bake at 450° for 15 minutes or until browned. **Yield:** 4 adult servings (serving size: about 4 ounces).

CALORIES 283; FAT 8.3g (sat 4.1g; mono 2.4g; poly 0.8g); PROTEIN 36.9g; CARB 14.2g; FIBER 1.9g; CHOL 80mg; IRON 2mg; SODIUM 710mg; CALC 278mg

Turkey and Bean Burrito

Refried beans help make a thick, hearty filling that's easy for toddlers to eat because it stays put. Serve the burritos for adults on a bed of lettuce topped with salsa and light sour cream.

let your toddler help by:

• Sprinkling the cheese on the tortillas.
• **Rolling up the tortillas.**

Cooking spray

8	ounces ground turkey
1½	tablespoons 40% less-sodium taco seasoning
¼	cup water
1	(16-ounce) can organic refried beans
⅓	cup salsa
6	(8-inch) whole-wheat flour tortillas
1	cup (4 ounces) preshredded reduced-fat Mexican blend cheese

1. Heat a large nonstick skillet over medium heat; coat pan with cooking spray. Add turkey to pan; cook 7 minutes or until turkey is done, stirring frequently. **2. Add** taco seasoning and ¼ cup water to pan, stirring well. Add beans and salsa, stirring gently to combine. Reduce heat to low, and cook 3 minutes or until thoroughly heated. **3. Warm** flour tortillas according to package directions. Sprinkle 2 tablespoons cheese down center of each tortilla; top each with about ⅓ cup turkey mixture. Roll up tortillas. **Yield:** 6 adult servings (serving size: 1 burrito).

CALORIES 264; FAT 12.4g (sat 2.9g, mono 1.3g, poly 1.5g); PROTEIN 20.6g; CARB 20.8g; FIBER 7.5g; CHOL 41mg; IRON 2.6mg; SODIUM 764mg; CALC 260mg

Five-Cheese Spinach Calzones

Calzones are easy to make, taste great, and pack a lot of calcium. Serve them with fresh fruit for a complete meal.

let your toddler help by:

- Patting the dough into a rectangle.
- Sprinkling the mozzarella and cheddar cheeses over the spinach mixture.

¾ cup 1% low-fat cottage cheese
½ cup light sour cream
¼ cup (2 ounces) ⅓-less-fat cream cheese
3 tablespoons grated fresh Parmesan cheese
1 (10-ounce) package frozen chopped spinach, thawed, drained, and squeezed dry
1 (12-ounce) bottle roasted red bell peppers, drained and chopped
1 teaspoon garlic powder
¼ teaspoon freshly ground black pepper
1 (13.8-ounce) can refrigerated pizza crust dough
Cooking spray
¼ cup (1 ounce) shredded part-skim mozzarella cheese
¼ cup (1 ounce) shredded reduced-fat sharp cheddar cheese
1½ cups bottled tomato-basil pasta sauce (optional)

1. **Preheat** oven to 425°. 2. **Combine** first 4 ingredients; beat with a mixer at medium speed 1 minute or until well blended. Stir in spinach and next 3 ingredients. 3. **Unroll** pizza dough onto a baking sheet coated with cooking spray; pat into a 14 x 10–inch rectangle. Spread spinach mixture over half of crust, leaving a 1-inch border. Sprinkle mozzarella and cheddar cheeses over spinach mixture. Fold dough over filling; press edges together to seal. 4. **Bake** at 425° for 17 minutes or until browned. Cool on a wire rack 5 minutes. Heat pasta sauce in a small saucepan over medium heat.

Cut calzone into 6 portions, and serve with pasta sauce, if desired. **Yield:** 6 adult servings (serving size: 1 calzone piece).

CALORIES 294; FAT 9g (sat 5g, mono 0.4g, poly 0.1g); PROTEIN 16.1g; CARB 38.6g; FIBER 1.5g; CHOL 23mg; IRON 2.8mg; SODIUM 908mg; CALC 216mg

Chicken and Root Vegetable Potpie

You can also bake this recipe in individual (10-ounce) ramekins for the same amount of time. Toddlers will love having their own potpie—just make sure you let the ramekins cool completely before serving.

let your toddler help by:

- Identifying and locating the vegetables.
- Helping roll the dough.

3 cups fat-free, less-sodium chicken broth
1½ cups frozen green peas, thawed
1 cup (½-inch) cubed peeled baking potato
1 cup (½-inch) cubed peeled sweet potato
1 cup (½-inch) cubed peeled celeriac
1 cup (½-inch-thick) slices parsnip
1 (10-ounce) package frozen pearl onions
1 pound skinless, boneless chicken breasts, cut into bite-sized pieces
3 ounces all-purpose flour (about ⅔ cup), divided
1½ cups fat-free milk
¼ cup chopped fresh parsley
2 tablespoons chopped fresh thyme
1½ teaspoons salt
1 teaspoon freshly ground black pepper
Cooking spray
1 sheet frozen puff pastry dough, thawed

A healthy balance

I've always tried to live a healthy lifestyle, but having a baby raised the bar. When I should have been catching up on sleep, I made all of my own whole-food, fresh, steamed baby food, and then I began cooking my son meals with whole grains and seasonal produce. My husband and I wanted nothing but nutritionally superior food for our kid, but we harbored a dark little secret: Oreo® cookies. We love them. Really love them. I complain loudly about him buying them, but then I secretly sneak into the cupboard during hours when one should not be eating Oreos and eat Oreos. Eventually the hypocrisy became unbearable. I caved and gave my toddler one cookie. The funny thing was that he didn't act like it was his first Oreo. He reached out for it with a suspicious familiarity that made me wonder who'd been sneaking him sugar-filled treats. Lest you label me as extreme, let me explain: There has to be a balance. If you think too much about the potential detrimental effects of each and every thing you (and your children) eat, you'll drive yourself crazy and end up with a diet of brown rice and raw organic carrots. Life's too short not to eat Oreos.

—Kim Cross, mom of Austin, 21 months

---

1. Preheat oven to 400°. **2. Bring** broth to a boil in a large Dutch oven. Add peas and next 5 ingredients to pan; cover, reduce heat, and simmer for 6 minutes. Add chicken and cook 5 minutes or until chicken is done. Remove chicken and vegetables from broth with a slotted spoon and place in a large bowl.
3. Increase heat to medium. Weigh or lightly spoon flour into dry measuring cups; level with a knife. Place all but 1 tablespoon flour in a medium bowl; gradually add milk to bowl, stirring with a whisk until well blended. Add milk mixture to broth; cook for 5 minutes or until thickened, stirring frequently. Stir in chicken mixture, parsley, and next 3 ingredients. Spoon mixture into an 11 x 7-inch baking dish coated with cooking spray. **4. Sprinkle** remaining 1 tablespoon flour on a work surface; roll dough into a 13 x 9-inch rectangle. Place dough over chicken mixture, pressing dough to seal at edges of dish. Cut small slits into dough to allow steam to escape and coat dough lightly with cooking spray. Place dish on a foil-lined baking sheet. Bake at 400° for 16 minutes or until pastry is browned and filling is bubbly. **Yield:** 8 adult servings.

CALORIES 388; FAT 13g (sat 2g, mono 3g, poly 7.1g); PROTEIN 21.9g; CARB 45.7g; FIBER 4.4g; CHOL 34mg; IRON 3mg; SODIUM 790mg; CALC 115mg

Instead of guessing what your child wants to eat, involve her in the process. Stock your pantry with healthy items, and then give your toddler a small nonbreakable container, and let her pick her combination. These mixtures prevent boredom, satisfy your toddler's need for independence, and, on busy mornings, provide a nutritious breakfast that can be eaten on the go. See page 54 for information about choking hazards.

Here are suggested items to keep on hand:
- Whole-grain, low-sugar cereals
- Raisins, dried apricots, dried bananas, and other dried fruits
- Whole-grain cheddar crackers
- Air-popped popcorn
- Almonds, peanuts, cashews, and other nuts

Breakfast mix ideas:
- Low-fat granola, dried cranberries, and walnut pieces
- Whole-grain toasted Os, raisins, and oven-toasted cinnamon square cereal
- Low-fat granola, whole-grain toasted Os, almond slivers, and dried blueberries

Snack mix ideas:
- Popcorn, dried cranberries, and cashews
- Popcorn, whole-grain cheddar crackers, and raisins
- Whole-grain toasted Os, popcorn, and dried banana slices
- Whole-grain toasted Os, raisins, and whole-grain cheddar crackers

Whole-Wheat Pepperoni Pizza

let your toddler help by:
- Pouring the measured ingredients into the food processor with your guidance.
- Placing the pepperoni slices on the pizza.
- Sprinkling the cheese on the pizza.

3.6 ounces whole-wheat flour (about ¾ cup)
3.4 ounces all-purpose flour (about ¾ cup)
1 package quick-rise yeast (about 2¼ teaspoons)
½ teaspoon salt
½ teaspoon sugar
⅔ cup very warm water (120° to 130°)
1 tablespoon olive oil
Cooking spray
⅔ cup tomato-basil pasta sauce
24 slices turkey pepperoni
1½ cups (6 ounces) part-skim mozzarella cheese

1. Weigh or lightly spoon flours into dry measuring cups; level with a knife. Place flours, yeast, salt, and sugar in a food processor; process until blended. Combine very warm water and oil in a 1-cup glass measure. Slowly pour water mixture through food chute with processor on; process until mixture forms a ball. Process an additional 1 minute. **2. Turn** dough out onto a floured surface; coat dough with cooking spray. Let rest 15 minutes. **3. Preheat** oven to 500°. **4. Roll** dough into a 12-inch circle. Place dough on an inverted large baking sheet coated with cooking spray. Crimp edges of dough to form a rim. Spread sauce over surface of dough, leaving a ½-inch border; sprinkle sauce with pepperoni and cheese. **5. Bake** at 500° for 11 minutes or until cheese melts and crust is golden. Cut into 6 wedges. **Yield:** 6 adult servings (serving size: 1 wedge).

CALORIES 261; FAT 9.8g (sat 4.3g, mono 3.7g, poly 0.8g); PROTEIN 14.3g; CARB 29.4g; FIBER 2.7g; CHOL 25mg; IRON 1.8mg; SODIUM 602mg; CALC 235mg

Whole-Wheat Pepperoni Pizza

Apple-Date Bars

These offer a great homemade alternative to store-bought cereal bars. The butter contributes to the golden crust of the dense, moist fruit-studded treats. You can use walnuts instead of pecans or substitute raisins for the dates.

let your toddler help by:

- Locating and gathering the ingredients.
- Pouring the measured dry ingredients into the mixing bowl.
- Adding the measured dates, apples, and pecans to the batter.

9	ounces all-purpose flour (about 2 cups)
1	teaspoon baking soda
1	teaspoon baking powder
½	teaspoon ground cinnamon
¼	teaspoon salt
2	cups sugar
7	tablespoons butter, softened
1	large egg
2	large egg whites
¼	cup applesauce
1	teaspoon vanilla extract
1	cup chopped pitted dates
1	teaspoon all-purpose flour
1½	cups chopped peeled Granny Smith apple (about 1 large)
1½	cups chopped peeled Red Delicious apple (about 1 large)
½	teaspoon fresh lemon juice
⅔	cup chopped pecans

Cooking spray

1. Preheat oven to 325°. **2. Weigh** or lightly spoon 9 ounces flour into dry measuring cups; level with a knife. Combine flour and next 4 ingredients in a large bowl, stirring with a whisk. Set aside. **3. Place** sugar and butter in a large bowl, and beat with a mixer at high speed for 2 minutes or until light and fluffy. Add egg and egg whites, one at a time, beating well after each addition. Stir in applesauce and vanilla. Gradually add flour mixture to sugar mixture; stir just until combined to form a stiff batter. Toss dates with 1 teaspoon flour. Toss apples with juice. Add dates, apples, and pecans to flour mixture, stirring just until combined. Pour batter into a 13 x 9–inch baking dish coated with cooking spray. Bake at 325° for 1 hour and 5 minutes or until a wooden pick inserted in center comes out clean. Cool completely on a wire rack. **Yield:** 16 adult servings (serving size: 1 bar).

CALORIES 279; FAT 9g (sat 3.6g, mono 3.4g, poly 1.4g); PROTEIN 3.3g; CARB 48.5g; FIBER 2g; CHOL 26mg; IRON 1.1mg; SODIUM 193mg; CALC 33mg

kitchen tip

To help prevent spills, measure the ingredients, and then transfer them to a larger, nonbreakable container. Giving your toddler a larger container to pour the ingredients out of reduces the chance of spills.

Banana-Orange Pops

Teething tots will especially love these treats. We used 8 (½-cup) ice pop molds, but you can use small paper cups if you don't have molds.

let your toddler help by:

- Pouring the measured banana and orange into a bowl.
- Stirring together the ingredients.

2   cups mashed ripe banana (about 5 medium)
1   cup orange juice
1   teaspoon lemon juice

1. Combine all ingredients in a medium bowl; divide mixture evenly among ice pop molds. Cover and freeze 8 hours. **Yield:** 8 servings (serving size: 1 pop).

CALORIES 66; FAT 0.3g (sat 0.1g, mono 0g, poly 0g); PROTEIN 0.8g; CARB 16.5g; FIBER 1.4g; CHOL 0mg; IRON 0.2mg; SODIUM 1mg; CALC 7mg

Granola-Banana Bites

Toddlers can help assemble these small, fun-to-eat treats to enjoy for breakfast or a snack.

let your toddler help by:

- Sprinkling the granola over the peanut butter.

2   large bananas
2   tablespoons natural peanut butter
1   tablespoon honey
2   tablespoons granola

1. Peel and cut bananas into ¾-inch slices. **2. Combine** peanut butter and honey. Place granola in a food processer; pulse 3 to 4 times until finely chopped. Spread about ¼ teaspoon peanut butter mixture onto 1 cut side of each banana slice; sprinkle evenly with granola. **Yield:** 6 servings (serving size: 3 bites).

CALORIES 93; FAT 3.2g (sat 0.5g, mono 1.6g, poly 1g); PROTEIN 2g; CARB 16g; FIBER 1.7g; CHOL 0mg; IRON 0.3mg; SODIUM 18mg; CALC 7mg

Banana-Mango Frozen Yogurt

You can feel good about this dessert because it's made with fresh fruit, milk, and yogurt.

let your toddler help by:

- Pouring the measured fruit and sugar into the blender with your guidance.

1   cup sliced ripe banana
¾   cup chopped peeled mango
⅓   cup orange juice
3   tablespoons fresh lime juice
1½   cups 2% low-fat milk
¾   cup sugar
1   (16-ounce) carton vanilla low-fat yogurt

1. Place first 4 ingredients in a blender; process until smooth. Combine banana mixture, milk, sugar, and yogurt in a large bowl, stirring well with a whisk. **2. Pour** mixture into the freezer can of an ice-cream freezer; freeze according to manufacturer's instructions. Spoon into a freezer-safe container; cover and freeze at least 1 hour. **Yield:** 12 servings (serving size: ½ cup).

CALORIES 118; FAT 1.1g (sat 0.7g, mono 0.3g, poly 0.1g); PROTEIN 3.1g; CARB 24.9g; FIBER 0.5g; CHOL 4mg; IRON 0.1mg; SODIUM 41mg; CALC 105mg

Banana-Mango Frozen Yogurt

grocery shop talk

Some parents will do anything to avoid taking a toddler with them to the grocery store, but involving your child in the food shopping at this age also helps lay the beginnings of a foundation for a healthy diet. While at the store, talk with your toddler about what you are buying. "What kind of fruit should we get today? What should we cook for dinner tonight? Can you help me find the broccoli?" You can have similar conversations when unloading groceries at home. Let your child help put things away, and use the time to talk with your child about food. These kinds of conversations are also great ways to teach and reinforce counting and color-identification skills.

Fresh Cherry Smoothie

This smoothie is perfect for a cool snack or breakfast shake during summer months when cherries are ripe. Serve it to your toddler in a small nonbreakable glass with or without a straw.

let your toddler help by:

• Pouring the measured cherries, ice, and yogurt into the blender with your guidance.

1	cup pitted sweet cherries
¾	cup ice
¾	cup plain fat-free or low-fat yogurt
2	tablespoons honey

1. Place all ingredients in a blender; process until smooth. Serve immediately. **Yield:** 2 adult servings (serving size: 1 cup).

CALORIES 168; FAT 0.9g (sat 0.3g, mono 0.2g, poly 0.2g); PROTEIN 6.2g; CARB 36.5g; FIBER 1.7g; CHOL 2mg; IRON 0.5mg; SODIUM 72mg; CALC 195mg

Sunshine Smoothie

This slightly sweet, thick drink is a great snack or part of breakfast. You can also freeze it in ice pop molds for a refreshing—and nutritious—frozen treat.

let your toddler help by:

• Pouring the measured fruit and yogurt into the blender with your guidance.

½	cup chopped peeled mango
1½	cups chopped peeled apricots (about 4 small)
⅔	cup chopped peeled nectarine (about 1 medium)
1	cup chopped cantaloupe
¼	cup mango nectar (such as Jumex)
⅛	teaspoon grated lemon rind
1	(6-ounce) carton lemon low-fat yogurt
1	cup ice cubes

1. Place mango in a zip-top plastic bag; seal. Freeze 1 hour. **2. Place** chopped apricots and next 5 ingredients in a blender; process until smooth. Add frozen mango and ice; process until smooth. **Yield:** 4 adult servings (serving size: about 1 cup).

CALORIES 104; FAT 0.9g (sat 0.4g, mono 0.3g, poly 0.1g); PROTEIN 3.4g; CARB 22.5g; FIBER 3g; CHOL 2mg; IRON 0.4mg; SODIUM 36mg; CALC 86mg

Sunshine Smoothie

nutrition note

Just one serving offers
about one-third of the day's
vitamin C and vitamin A
needs for both parents
and toddlers.

special section

Lunch-Box Solutions; Holiday Helpers; and Happy Birthday, Baby!

Meals away from home and meals shared as part of a special occasion can be challenging for parents. Here are some ideas to provide your toddler with proper nutrition while still including her in the family fun.

lunch-box solutions

Finding nutritious lunch options that picky toddlers will eat is a challenge all parents face. We've got some new ideas that can be prepared in no time—whether you're packing them in lunch boxes the night before or trying to stave off starving toddlers for lunch at home.

PB&J Revisited

Using cinnamon-raisin bread puts a fresh touch on the traditional peanut butter and jelly sandwich.

for your toddler:

• Serve the sandwich with baby carrots and milk.

1 tablespoon natural peanut butter (such as Smucker's)
2 (1-ounce) slices whole-grain cinnamon-raisin bread
2 teaspoons any flavor of fruit spread (such as Polaner All-Fruit)

1. Spread peanut butter evenly on one side of a bread slice; spread fruit spread on one side of remaining bread slice. Press bread together, and cut into squares. **Yield:** 1 adult serving (serving size: 1 sandwich).

CALORIES 283; FAT 11g (sat 1.1g, mono 4g, poly 2.5g); PROTEIN 8g; CARB 40.7g; FIBER 3.1g; CHOL 0mg; IRON 1.8mg; SODIUM 235mg; CALC 9mg

kitchen tip

If you have trouble spreading natural peanut butter after it's been in the refrigerator, try warming a few tablespoons in the microwave for 15 seconds.

Mini PB&J Sandwiches variation: Use a slightly toasted whole-wheat mini bagel in place of the bread slices. Cut the sandwich in half before serving.

CALORIES 192; FAT 8.4g (sat 1.2g, mono 4g, poly 2.7g); PROTEIN 6.5g; CARB 24.6g; FIBER 1.7g; CHOL 0mg; IRON 1.4mg; SODIUM 126mg; CALC 14mg

Turkey Vegetable Wraps

This recipe makes two adult-sized wraps. Feed little one half of a wrap, and refrigerate the other half for tomorrow's lunch. Take the second wrap with you to work, or send it with an older sibling or your spouse. Feel free to omit the green onions, if desired.

for your toddler:

• Wrap it tightly so it will be easier for a toddler to eat.
• Refrigerate it until serving time, or pack it in an insulated bag.
• Serve it with grape halves and milk.

1 cup coarsely chopped deli turkey breast
1 cup mixed salad greens
¼ cup frozen whole kernel corn, thawed and drained
¼ cup chopped red bell pepper
2 tablespoons thinly sliced green onions
2 tablespoons light ranch dressing
2 (8-inch) whole-wheat flour tortillas

1. Combine first 6 ingredients in a large bowl, tossing well to coat. **2. Warm** tortillas according to package directions; top each tortilla with 1 cup turkey mixture. Roll up, and cut diagonally in half. **Yield:** 2 adult servings (serving size: 1 wrap).

CALORIES 201; FAT 8.3g (sat 0.3g, mono 0g, poly 0.1g); PROTEIN 17.5g; CARB 14.8g; FIBER 4.3g; CHOL 25mg; IRON 1.6mg; SODIUM 763mg; CALC 81mg

Turkey Vegetable Wraps

Guacamole Chicken Wraps

Lettuce leaves line the tortillas, keeping the wraps fresh. You can save time by using meat from a rotisserie chicken.

for your toddler:

• Wrap it tightly so it will be easier for a toddler to eat.
• Refrigerate it until serving time, or pack it in an insulated bag.
• Serve it with natural applesauce and milk.

2	tablespoons fresh lime juice
¼	teaspoon salt
1	ripe peeled avocado
½	cup chopped seeded plum tomato
4	green leaf lettuce leaves
4	(8-inch) whole-wheat flour tortillas
2	cups shredded skinless, boneless cooked chicken breast

1. Place first 3 ingredients in a medium bowl; mash with a fork until smooth. Stir in tomato. **2. Place** 1 lettuce leaf on each tortilla; spread about ¼ cup avocado mixture on each leaf. Top each serving with ½ cup chicken. Roll up. Wrap in foil or parchment paper; chill. **Yield:** 4 adult servings (serving size: 1 wrap).

CALORIES 249; FAT 11.8g (sat 1.5g, mono 4.1g, poly 1.2g); PROTEIN 26.8g; CARB 11.6g; FIBER 5.1g; CHOL 60mg; IRON 2mg; SODIUM 466mg; CALC 80mg

rotisserie chicken

Rotisserie chicken is great to keep on hand for a quick meal. When buying rotisserie chicken at the grocery store, pick it up at the end of your shopping trip so it stays hot until you get it home. Serve or refrigerate it within two hours or sooner in hot weather. It'll keep in the refrigerator for three to four days.

Chicken, Rice, and Tropical Fruit Salad

Serve this salad chilled or at room temperature, depending on your preference. You can substitute lime juice for lemon, if you'd like.

for your toddler:

• Omit the lettuce leaf.
• Place a spoonful of the salad in a small bowl or resealable plastic dish.
• Refrigerate it until serving time, or pack it in an insulated bag.
• Serve it with whole-wheat crackers, cucumber slices, and milk.
• Remember to pack a spoon or fork.

1	cup uncooked basmati rice
2	cups cubed skinless, boneless rotisserie chicken breast
1	cup cubed fresh pineapple
1	cup jarred sliced peeled mango, drained and chopped (such as Del Monte SunFresh)
½	cup seedless red grapes, halved
¼	cup sliced almonds, toasted
2	tablespoons finely chopped fresh mint
1½	tablespoons fresh lemon juice
1½	tablespoons canola oil
¼	teaspoon salt
4	romaine lettuce leaves

1. Cook rice according to package directions, omitting salt and fat. Cool. Combine rice and next 5 ingredients. **2. Combine** mint and next 3 ingredients in a small bowl, stirring with a whisk. Drizzle mint mixture over rice mixture; toss well. Cover and chill. Place 1 lettuce leaf on each of four plates. Spoon 1½ cups rice mixture onto each lettuce leaf. **Yield:** 4 adult servings.

CALORIES 346; FAT 11.5g (sat 1.4g, mono 6.2g, poly 3g); PROTEIN 25.5g; CARB 36.1g; FIBER 2.8g; CHOL 60mg; IRON 1.6mg; SODIUM 199mg; CALC 45mg

Chicken, Rice,
and Tropical Fruit Salad

holiday helpers

The usual holiday meal may leave few options for baby, so we've created a menu that's sure to satisfy and nourish both little ones and adults.

Simple Baked Ham

Because the seasonings are mild, this ham is good for dinner or breakfast. Soaking the ham in water draws out some of the sodium, leaving the ham less salty.

for your toddler:

• Cut a small serving of ham into bite-sized pieces.
• Serve the pieces of ham with a fork or as finger food with side dishes.

1   (8-pound) 33%-less-sodium smoked, fully cooked ham half
2   teaspoons whole cloves
Cooking spray
2   cups apple juice, divided
2   tablespoons dark brown sugar
1   tablespoon Dijon mustard

1. **Place** ham in a large Dutch oven or stockpot. Cover with water to 2 inches above ham; cover and refrigerate for 24 hours. Drain; rinse well with warm water. Drain. 2. **Preheat** oven to 325°. 3. **Trim** fat and rind from ham. Score outside of ham in a diamond pattern; stud with cloves. Place ham, skin side down, on the rack of a broiler pan coated with cooking spray. Place rack in pan; pour 1 cup apple juice over ham. Cover ham loosely with foil. Bake at 325° for 2½ hours, basting occasionally with remaining 1 cup apple juice. 4. **Remove** ham from oven (do not turn oven off); uncover ham. Combine sugar and mustard; brush over ham. Bake, uncovered, at 325° for 30 minutes or until a thermometer inserted into thickest portion registers 140°. Place ham on a cutting board; cover and let stand 10 minutes before slicing. **Yield:** 26 adult servings (serving size: about 3 ounces).

CALORIES 130; FAT 6.3g (sat 2.1g, mono 3g, poly 0.7g); PROTEIN 14.6g; CARB 3.5g; FIBER 0g; CHOL 52mg; IRON 0.8mg; SODIUM 819mg; CALC 2mg

Mashed Sweet Potatoes with Pecan Butter

The pecan-butter mixture elevates this simple side dish to holiday worthiness. Microwaving the potatoes makes preparation a cinch and frees up your oven for the main dish.

for your toddler:

• Serve a spoonful of the potatoes on a plate or in a small bowl with a spoon.
• Omit the pecan-butter mixture, if desired.

6   sweet potatoes (about 3 pounds)
2   tablespoons water
¾   cup 1% low-fat milk
6   tablespoons light brown sugar, divided
½   teaspoon salt
3   tablespoons butter, softened
3   tablespoons chopped pecans, toasted
½   teaspoon ground cinnamon

1. **Place** potatoes and water in a medium bowl; cover bowl with plastic wrap. Microwave at HIGH

10 minutes or until tender; let cool slightly. Scoop out pulp, discarding skins. Combine sweet potato, milk, 3 tablespoons brown sugar, and salt in a medium bowl; mash with a potato masher to desired consistency. **2. Combine** remaining 3 tablespoons brown sugar, butter, pecans, and cinnamon in a small bowl. Sprinkle butter mixture evenly over potato mixture. **Yield:** 6 adult servings (serving size: ¾ cup sweet potatoes and about 2 teaspoons pecan butter).

CALORIES 276; FAT 8.9g (sat 4.1g, mono 3.1g, poly 1.2g); PROTEIN 3.8g; CARB 46.9g; FIBER 4.9g; CHOL 16mg; IRON 1.7mg; SODIUM 303mg; CALC 104mg

Spinach and Parmesan Fallen Soufflé

Squeezing the cooked spinach removes excess moisture. Double the recipe for a larger crowd.

for your toddler:

• Serve a spoonful of the soufflé on a plate or in a small bowl with a spoon.

Cooking spray

2	tablespoons dry breadcrumbs
2	garlic cloves, minced
10	ounces fresh spinach
1	cup 1% low-fat milk
1	tablespoon cornstarch
⅓	cup (about 1½ ounces) grated fresh Parmigiano-Reggiano cheese
¼	teaspoon salt
⅛	teaspoon freshly ground black pepper
⅛	teaspoon grated whole nutmeg
3	large egg whites
1	large egg

1. Preheat oven to 375°. **2. Lightly** coat an 11 x 7–inch baking dish with cooking spray, and dust with bread-crumbs. Set aside. **3. Heat** a large nonstick skillet over medium heat; coat pan with cooking spray. Add garlic and cook 20 seconds, stirring constantly. Add spinach and cook 3 minutes or until spinach wilts, stirring occasionally. Remove from heat; cool slightly. Place spinach mixture on several layers of heavy-duty paper towels, and squeeze until barely moist. Place spinach mixture in a blender. Add milk and cornstarch; process until smooth. Add cheese and next 3 ingredients; pulse until well blended. Pour into a large bowl. **4. Place** egg whites and egg in a large bowl; beat with a mixer at high speed 5 minutes or until tripled in volume. Gently fold one-fourth of egg mixture into spinach mixture; gently fold in remaining egg mixture (mixture will seem slightly thin). Spoon spinach-egg mixture into prepared baking dish, and smooth top with a spatula. **5. Bake** at 375° for 35 minutes or until center is set. Cool 5 minutes on a wire rack before serving. **Yield:** 6 adult servings (serving size: ⅙ of casserole).

CALORIES 92; FAT 3.5g (sat 1.8g, mono 1g, poly 0.3g); PROTEIN 8.5g; CARB 7.3g; FIBER 1.2g; CHOL 42mg; IRON 1.7mg; SODIUM 326mg; CALC 193mg

nutrition note

holiday meals

dults associate holidays with special dishes and treats that they splurge on one time a year. It's important to remember, however, that toddlers don't have these food-holiday associations. To help keep your tot happy and healthy during the holidays, stick to his normal mealtimes, offer healthy food options, and limit the amount of high-calorie and high-fat foods you give him.

Gingerbread People

Use a variety of cookie cutter sizes to create "families." If you don't want to cut the dough into shapes, roll it into two logs, cover, chill, and slice into ⅛-inch rounds.

for your toddler:

- Serve the cookies plain or decorated.
- Let your toddler help mix the measured ingredients and decorate the cookies.

Cookies:

10	ounces all-purpose flour (about 2¼ cups)
1½	teaspoons ground ginger
1	teaspoon ground cinnamon
½	teaspoon baking powder
¼	teaspoon baking soda
¼	teaspoon salt
¼	teaspoon ground nutmeg
¼	teaspoon ground cloves
¾	cup granulated sugar
¼	cup butter, softened
½	cup molasses
1	large egg

Decorations:

1¼	cups powdered sugar
2	tablespoons 2% milk
¼	cup colored sugar sprinkles

kitchen tip

The holidays can be hectic, and these cookies can easily be made ahead. You can prepare the dough and refrigerate it for up to three days or freeze it for up to one month.

1. To prepare cookies, weigh or lightly spoon flour into dry measuring cups; level with a knife. Combine flour and next 7 ingredients in a large bowl, stirring with a whisk. **2. Place** granulated sugar and butter in a large bowl; beat with a mixer at medium speed until smooth and well blended. Add molasses and egg; beat until well blended. Stir flour mixture into granulated sugar mixture until well blended. Divide dough in half; shape each dough portion into a flat disk. Wrap dough portions separately in plastic wrap; chill 1 hour or until firm. **3. Preheat** oven to 350°. **4. Remove** 1 dough portion from refrigerator; remove plastic wrap. Roll dough to a ⅛-inch thickness on a floured surface. Cut with a 3-inch boy or girl cookie cutter. Place cookies ½ inch apart on parchment paper–lined baking sheets. Repeat procedure with remaining dough portion. Bake at 350° for 11 minutes or until edges of cookies are lightly browned. Remove from pans; cool completely on wire racks. **5. To prepare** decorations, combine powdered sugar and milk, stirring until smooth. Spoon mixture into a heavy-duty zip-top plastic bag. Snip a tiny hole in 1 corner of bag. Pipe onto cookies. Decorate as desired with sugar sprinkles. **Yield:** About 5 dozen cookies (serving size: 1 cookie).

CALORIES 56; FAT 0.9g (sat 0.5g, mono 0.2g, poly 0.1g); PROTEIN 0.6g; CARB 11.5g; FIBER 0.2g; CHOL 6mg; IRON 0.4mg; SODIUM 27mg; CALC 10mg

Gingerbread People

happy birthday, baby!

Although we don't advocate giving little ones sugar every day, we think birthdays are definitely worth the splurge. The following pages give you several tasty cake options that are moderate in fat and sugar and perfectly acceptable for celebrating baby's first few birthdays.

Banana Cupcakes with Cream Cheese Frosting

If the frosting is too thin, place it in the refrigerator for 30 minutes or until it is spreadable.

Cupcakes:

Cooking spray

4.5 ounces all-purpose flour (about 1 cup)

½ teaspoon baking soda

¼ teaspoon salt

¼ teaspoon ground nutmeg

¾ cup granulated sugar, divided

½ cup mashed ripe banana

¼ cup butter, softened

1 teaspoon vanilla extract

2 large eggs

¼ cup plain fat-free yogurt

Frosting:

½ cup (4 ounces) ⅓-less-fat cream cheese

½ teaspoon vanilla extract

1¾ cups powdered sugar, sifted

2 tablespoons finely chopped walnuts, toasted (optional)

1. Preheat oven to 350°. **2. To prepare** cupcakes, place muffin cup liners in 12 muffin cups. Coat each paper liner with cooking spray. **3. Weigh** or lightly spoon flour into a dry measuring cup; level with a knife. Combine flour and next 3 ingredients in a small bowl, stirring with a whisk. **4. Combine** ¼ cup granulated sugar and banana in a small bowl; set aside. Combine remaining ½ cup granulated sugar, butter, and vanilla in a large bowl; beat with a mixer at high speed until well blended. Add eggs, 1 at a time, beating well after each addition. Add banana mixture to sugar mixture, beating well. Add flour mixture and yogurt alternately to sugar mixture, beginning and ending with flour mixture. **5. Spoon** batter evenly into prepared muffin cups. Bake at 350° for 24 minutes or until a wooden pick inserted in center comes out clean. Cool in pan 10 minutes on a wire rack, and remove cupcakes from pan. Cool completely on a wire rack. **6. To prepare** frosting, combine cream cheese and vanilla in a large bowl; beat with a mixer at medium speed until smooth. Gradually add powdered sugar, beating just until smooth. Spread about 1 tablespoon frosting onto each cupcake. Sprinkle each cupcake with toasted walnuts, if desired. **Yield:** 12 servings (serving size: 1 cupcake).

CALORIES 244; FAT 7.4g (sat 4.1g, mono 1.4g, poly 0.9g); PROTEIN 3.7g; CARB 41.2g; FIBER 0.6g; CHOL 47mg; IRON 0.7mg; SODIUM 185mg; CALC 22mg

Banana Cupcakes with
Cream Cheese Frosting

Happy Birthday, Baby! **133**

Yellow Cake
with Chocolate Frosting

Yellow Cake with Chocolate Frosting

By dividing the cake batter between two pans, this recipe allows you to make an individual cake for baby and a larger one for adults to enjoy.

Cake:

Cooking spray

1½   tablespoons all-purpose flour

¾   cup butter, melted

1¼   cups fat-free sour cream

2¼   cups granulated sugar

1   tablespoon vanilla extract

2   large eggs

2   large egg whites

13.5   ounces all-purpose flour (about 3 cups)

1½   teaspoons baking soda

¾   teaspoon salt

1   cup plus 2 tablespoons low-fat buttermilk

Frosting:

¾   cup (6 ounces) ⅓-less-fat cream cheese, softened

6   tablespoons butter, softened

1½   teaspoons vanilla extract

⅓   cup unsweetened cocoa

2   tablespoons fat-free milk

⅛   teaspoon salt

4½   cups powdered sugar

1. Preheat oven to 350°. **2. To prepare** cake, coat bottom of a 13 x 9–inch baking pan and an 8-inch square baking pan with cooking spray (do not coat sides of pans); line bottoms of pans with wax paper. Coat wax paper with cooking spray; dust pans with 1½ tablespoons flour. Set aside. **3. Combine** ¾ cup butter and sour cream in a large bowl, stirring with a whisk until well blended. Add granulated sugar and 1 tablespoon vanilla. Beat with a mixer at medium speed 3 minutes or until well blended. Add eggs and egg whites, 1 at a time, to sugar mixture, beating well after each addition. **4. Weigh** or lightly spoon 13.5 ounces flour (about 3 cups) into dry measuring cups; level with a knife. Combine 13.5 ounces flour, baking soda, and ¾ teaspoon salt in a large bowl, stirring with a whisk. Add flour mixture and buttermilk alternately to sugar mixture, beginning and ending with flour mixture. **5. Pour** about two-thirds of batter into 13 x 9–inch pan; pour remaining batter into 8-inch square pan. Sharply tap pans once on counter to remove air bubbles. Bake at 350° for 30 minutes or until a wooden pick inserted in center comes out clean. Cool in pans on a wire rack for 10 minutes. Remove from pans; cool completely on wire racks. **6. To prepare** frosting, place cream cheese, 6 tablespoons butter, and 1½ teaspoons vanilla in a large bowl; beat with a mixer at medium speed until fluffy. Add cocoa, milk, and ⅛ teaspoon salt; beat at low speed until blended. Gradually add powdered sugar, beating until well combined. **7. To prepare** baby cake, cut 2 (4-inch) circles out of 8-inch square cake. Place 1 cake layer on a small plate; spread with 3 tablespoons frosting. Top with remaining cake layer. Spread ¾ cup plus 1 tablespoon frosting over top and sides of cake. **8. To prepare** adult cake, place 13 x 9–inch cake on a serving platter; spread 2 cups frosting on top and sides of cake. Store cakes loosely covered in refrigerator. **Yield:** 1 baby cake and 1 adult cake (serving size: ¹⁄₁₆ of adult cake).

CALORIES 343; FAT 10.9g (sat 6.7g, mono 2.5g, poly 0.5g); PROTEIN 4.9g; CARB 57.5g; FIBER 0.8g; CHOL 48mg; IRON 1mg; SODIUM 290mg; CALC 55mg

Carrot Cake with Cream Cheese Frosting

Baby's first birthday is a special event to share with family and friends. This recipe makes one regular-sized layer cake for guests as well as a smaller cake just for baby.

Cake:

Cooking spray

3   tablespoons all-purpose flour

11.2 ounces all-purpose flour (about 2½ cups)

2   teaspoons baking powder

1½   teaspoons ground cinnamon

½   teaspoon salt

¼   teaspoon baking soda

¼   teaspoon ground nutmeg

⅓   cup granulated sugar

⅔   cup packed dark brown sugar

½   cup applesauce

⅓   cup canola oil

¼   cup vanilla low-fat yogurt

2½   teaspoons vanilla extract

2   large egg whites

1   large egg

2   cups finely shredded carrot (about 6 small)

Frosting:

3   tablespoons butter, softened

12   ounces ⅓-less-fat cream cheese, softened

4½   cups powdered sugar

2   teaspoons vanilla extract

1. Preheat oven to 350°. **2. To prepare** cake, coat 2 (8-inch) round and 1 (8-inch) square cake pans with cooking spray; dust with 3 tablespoons flour. Weigh or lightly spoon 11.2 ounces flour (about 2½ cups) into dry measuring cups; level with a knife. Combine flour, baking powder, and next 4 ingredients in a large bowl, stirring with a whisk. Combine granulated sugar and next 7 ingredients in a medium bowl; beat well with a mixer at medium speed. Stir in carrot. Add to flour mixture, stirring just until moist. **3. Pour** 1⅓ cups batter into each prepared pan. Bake at 350° for 20 minutes or until a wooden pick inserted in center comes out clean. Run a knife around outside edge of pans. Cool in pans 10 minutes on a wire rack; remove from pans. Cool completely on wire racks. **4. To prepare** frosting, combine butter and cream cheese in a large bowl. Beat with a mixer at medium speed until smooth. Gradually beat in powdered sugar and vanilla just until smooth. Cover and refrigerate until ready to use. **5. For baby's cake,** cut 2 small layers from square layer, using a (4-inch) round cookie cutter, discarding scraps. Place 1 layer on a small plate; spread with ⅓ cup frosting. Top with remaining layer. Spread ½ cup frosting on top and sides of cake. **6. For adult cake,** place 1 round cake layer on a plate; spread with ½ cup frosting. Top with remaining round layer. Spread 2¼ cups frosting on top and sides of cake. Store cakes loosely covered in refrigerator.

Yield: 1 baby cake and 1 adult cake (serving size: ¹⁄₁₆ of adult cake).

CALORIES 286; FAT 8.7g (sat 3.7g, mono 2.4g, poly 1.1g); PROTEIN 4.1g; CARB 48.3g; FIBER 0.8g; CHOL 26mg; IRON 1mg; SODIUM 207mg; CALC 54mg

kitchen tip

Shred your own carrots to ensure a moist, tender cake.

-To change to whole
wheat flour, add
a tbsp or 2 of liquid
↳applesauce?

baby and toddler tasting panel

All of the recipes in this book were tasted by our panel of baby and toddler tasters, who ranged in age from 6 months to 2½ years. We'd like to thank them, as well as their parents, for taking the time to participate in this book and providing us with invaluable feedback about each of these recipes that helped *Cooking Light First Foods* become the book that it is. *Not pictured:* Emma

Austin

Henry

James

Mills

Sedgie

David

John Paul

Porter

Elliott

Ben

Madeline

Wyatt

seasonal produce guide

When you use fresh fruits, vegetables, and herbs, you don't have to do much to make them taste great. Although many fruits, vegetables, and herbs are available year-round, you'll get better flavor and prices when you buy what's in season. The Seasonal Produce Guide below helps you choose the best produce so you can create sensational meals all year long.

spring

Fruits
Bananas
Blood oranges
Coconuts
Grapefruit
Kiwifruit
Lemons
Limes
Mangoes
Navel oranges
Papayas
Passion fruit
Pineapples
Strawberries
Tangerines
Valencia oranges

Vegetables
Artichokes
Arugula
Asparagus
Avocados
Baby leeks
Beets
Belgian endive
Broccoli
Cauliflower
Dandelion
  greens
Fava beans
Green onions
Green peas
Kale
Lettuce
Mushrooms
Radishes
Red potatoes
Rhubarb
Snap beans
Snow peas
Spinach
Sugar snap peas
Sweet onions
Swiss chard

Herbs
Chives
Dill
Garlic chives
Lemongrass
Mint
Parsley
Thyme

summer

Fruits
Blackberries
Blueberries
Boysenberries
Cantaloupes
Casaba melons
Cherries
Crenshaw melons
Grapes
Guava
Honeydew melons
Mangoes
Nectarines
Papayas
Peaches
Plums
Raspberries
Strawberries
Watermelons

Vegetables
Avocados
Beets
Bell peppers
Cabbage
Carrots
Celery
Chili peppers
Collards
Corn
Cucumbers
Eggplant
Green beans
Jicama
Lima beans
Okra
Pattypan squash
Peas
Radicchio
Radishes
Summer squash
Tomatoes

Herbs
Basil
Bay leaves
Borage
Chives
Cilantro
Dill
Lavender
Lemon balm
Marjoram
Mint
Oregano
Rosemary
Sage
Summer savory
Tarragon
Thyme

autumn

Fruits
Apples
Cranberries
Figs
Grapes
Pears
Persimmons
Pomegranates
Quinces

Vegetables
Belgian endive
Bell peppers
Broccoli
Brussels
  sprouts
Cabbage
Cauliflower
Eggplant
Escarole
Fennel
Frisée
Leeks
Mushrooms
Parsnips
Pumpkins
Red potatoes
Rutabagas
Shallots
Sweet potatoes
Winter squash
Yukon gold
  potatoes

Herbs
Basil
Bay leaves
Parsley
Rosemary
Sage
Tarragon
Thyme

winter

Fruits
Apples
Blood oranges
Cranberries
Grapefruit
Kiwifruit
Kumquats
Lemons
Limes
Mandarin oranges
Navel oranges
Pears
Persimmons
Pomegranates
Pomelos
Quinces
Tangelos
Tangerines

Vegetables
Baby turnips
Beets
Belgian endive
Brussels
  sprouts
Celery root
Chili peppers
Dried beans
Escarole
Fennel
Frisée
Jerusalem
  artichokes
Kale
Leeks
Mushrooms
Parsnips
Potatoes
Rutabagas
Sweet potatoes
Turnips
Watercress
Winter squash

Herbs
Bay leaves
Chives
Parsley
Rosemary
Sage
Thyme

nutritional analysis
How to use it and why

While *Cooking Light First Foods* is about feeding your child, many of the recipes are designed for the whole family to enjoy. With this in mind, we've included a full nutritional analysis at the end of each adult-appropriate *Cooking Light* recipe. With chefs, registered dietitians, home economists, and a computer system that analyzes every ingredient we use, *Cooking Light* gives you authoritative dietary detail. We go to such lengths so you can see how our recipes fit into your healthful eating plan.

Here's a helpful guide to put our nutritional analysis numbers into perspective. Remember, one size doesn't fit all, so take your lifestyle, age, and circumstances into consideration when determining your nutrition needs. For example, pregnant or breast-feeding women need more protein, calories, and calcium. And women older than 50 need 1,200mg of calcium daily, 200mg more than the amount recommended for younger women. Go to mypyramid.gov for your own individualized plan.

In our nutritional analysis, we use these abbreviations

sat	saturated fat	CHOL	cholesterol
mono	monounsaturated fat	CALC	calcium
poly	polyunsaturated fat	g	gram
CARB	carbohydrates	mg	milligram

Daily nutrition guide

	Women Ages 25 to 50	Women over 50	Men over 24
Calories	2,000	2,000 or less	2,700
Protein	50g	50g or less	63g
Fat	65g or less	65g or less	88g or less
Saturated Fat	20g or less	20g or less	27g or less
Carbohydrates	304g	304g	410g
Fiber	25g to 35g	25g to 35g	25g to 35g
Cholesterol	300mg or less	300mg or less	300mg or less
Iron	18mg	8mg	8mg
Sodium	2,300mg or less	1,500mg or less	2,300mg or less
Calcium	1,000mg	1,200mg	1,000mg

The nutritional values used in our calculations either come from The Food Processor, Version 8.9 (ESHA Research), or are provided by food manufacturers.

metric equivalents

The information in the following charts is provided to help cooks outside the United States successfully use the recipes in this book. All equivalents are approximate.

Cooking/oven temperatures

	Fahrenheit	Celsius	Gas Mark
Freeze Water	32° F	0° C	
Room Temp.	68° F	20° C	
Boil Water	212° F	100° C	
Bake	325° F	160° C	3
	350° F	180° C	4
	375° F	190° C	5
	400° F	200° C	6
	425° F	220° C	7
	450° F	230° C	8
Broil			Grill

Liquid ingredients by volume

¼ tsp	=	1 ml				
½ tsp	=	2 ml				
1 tsp	=	5 ml				
3 tsp	=	1 tbl	=	½ fl oz	=	15 ml
2 tbls	=	⅛ cup	=	1 fl oz	=	30 ml
4 tbls	=	¼ cup	=	2 fl oz	=	60 ml
5⅓ tbls	=	⅓ cup	=	3 fl oz	=	80 ml
8 tbls	=	½ cup	=	4 fl oz	=	120 ml
10⅔ tbls	=	⅔ cup	=	5 fl oz	=	160 ml
12 tbls	=	¾ cup	=	6 fl oz	=	180 ml
16 tbls	=	1 cup	=	8 fl oz	=	240 ml
1 pt	=	2 cups	=	16 fl oz	=	480 ml
1 qt	=	4 cups	=	32 fl oz	=	960 ml
				33 fl oz	= 1000 ml	= 1 l

Dry ingredients by weight

To convert ounces to grams, multiply the number of ounces by 30.

1 oz	=	¹⁄₁₆ lb	=	30 g
4 oz	=	¼ lb	=	120 g
8 oz	=	½ lb	=	240 g
12 oz	=	¾ lb	=	360 g
16 oz	=	1 lb	=	480 g

Length

To convert inches to centimeters, multiply the number of inches by 2.5.

1 in	=			2.5 cm	
6 in	=	½ ft	=	15 cm	
12 in	=	1 ft	=	30 cm	
36 in	=	3 ft	= 1 yd =	90 cm	
40 in	=			100 cm	= 1m

Equivalents for different types of ingredients

Standard Cup	Fine Powder (ex. flour)	Grain (ex. rice)	Granular (ex. sugar)	Liquid Solids (ex. butter)	Liquid (ex. milk)
1	140 g	150 g	190 g	200 g	240 ml
¾	105 g	113 g	143 g	150 g	180 ml
⅔	93 g	100 g	125 g	133 g	160 ml
½	70 g	75 g	95 g	100 g	120 ml
⅓	47 g	50 g	63 g	67 g	80 ml
¼	35 g	38 g	48 g	50 g	60 ml
⅛	18 g	19 g	24 g	25 g	30 ml

Recipe Index

Subject Index